# LEADERSHIP ROLES ARE ~~NOT~~ FOR WOMEN

## A BOOK FOR MINDFUL LEADERS



KAVITHA RAMAKRISHNAPPA

INDIA · SINGAPORE · MALAYSIA

ISBN 979-8-89475-355-3



I have drawn upon various internet references to highlight key points to provide clarity on the topic. All credit goes to the respective authors. Utilizing these references has been instrumental in thoughtfully structuring this book.

# DEDICATION

I dedicate this book to my mother, Shantha KN,
who has not only nurtured me but also instilled in me
the values of integrity, honesty, and transparency,
and most importantly, taught me to stand up
for myself and others whenever needed.

–Love you, Amma 

# # GRATITUDE #

To my Parents, my Sister, my Brother,
my Husband & my Son – you all mean the world to me.
Your guidance, help and support has shaped me into a
better person every day.

I would like to express my heartfelt gratitude to the
leaders who have provided me with equal opportunities
and guided me to become a better leader throughout my
professional journey.

# CONTENTS

# PREFACE

Every book has its genesis in a spark—a moment of clarity that compels an author to transform thought into words. For me, that spark was ignited in the corporate boardrooms and hallways where ambition meets tradition. Time and again, I witnessed incredibly capable women doubt their rightful place in leadership roles, held back not by a lack of skill, but by pervasive and outdated beliefs. This is why I wrote this book.

My career began not at the top, but as one among many, navigating the intricacies of corporate life as an individual contributor. As I climbed the corporate ladder, the landscape at higher levels was starkly different—few or no women held positions of power or titles. It became clear that the issue wasn't about ability; it was about perception. Women often is into leadership role at home, seamlessly managing complex family dynamics and decisions. Yet, translating these inherent skills into the workplace requires not just ability, which is abundant, but confidence, which is often eroded by societal norms.

This book is for the young and the experienced alike for anyone who has felt their potential was a whisper in a storm of doubt. It is for everyone who have been told, directly or indirectly, that leadership role is out of reach.

Here, I share not just my story, but also the stories of those who have paved their way through doubt and adversity. Through inspiring narratives, practical advice, and humor, I aim to mentor you as you navigate your own path. This book will equip you with essential skills with the right mindset, and how to adapt to changing circumstances. More importantly, it will teach you to embrace failure as a stepping stone to success, to say no when it matters, and to harness the power of silence.

I hope that by the final page, you feel you've gained more than just a mentor in print. My aim is for this book to serve as a continual guide, a source of encouragement, and a beacon of possibility. You should not only feel equipped to advance in your career but also inspire to mentor others along their paths.

As you turn these pages, let each story and piece of advice build your confidence and affirm your capacity to lead. Let this book be your push to challenge the status quo and to step boldly into the roles you deserve. After all, true leadership is about making an impact—let's make it together.

# ACKNOWLEDGMENTS

This book is a tribute to my parents, Mr. Ramakrishnappa and Mrs. Shantha.

I extend my heartfelt gratitude to my elder sister, Manjula Ramakrishnappa, and my elder brother, Rajesh Ramakrishnappa for making my journey from childhood to adulthood fun, meaningful and worthwhile.

To my husband, Deepak, and my son, Jeevan, I express my deepest love and admiration. Blessed to receive their unwavering support and unconditional love that has made my life truly fulfilling.

*"Great leaders don't set out to be a leader... they set out to make a difference. It's never about the role—always about the goal."*

– Lisa Haisha

## CHAPTER 1

# WHY SHOULD YOU BECOME A LEADER & HOW?

After being the top performer at my company for 1.5 years, I was promoted to the next level. It was a moment of pride and accomplishment. But when I saw the organizational chart, I noticed something odd. One of my team members was not reporting to me. Instead, he was reporting directly to my boss.

Curious and a bit confused, I asked why this person not reporting to me although he is still part of my team. Guess what was the response? He would be uncomfortable if he had to report to me. He wouldn't handle it well reporting to a woman, let alone someone he saw as a peer and friend.

So, the solution was to let him report directly to the VP. I was basically told that's just the way it would have to be. And sadly, I've seen behavior like this tolerated many times in my career.

Here's the thing: In this case, the man needed a training for mindset shift, but because of such men women are going through empowerment programs. When decisions like this are made, it permits people to keep behaving badly instead of supporting the rest of the team. Men, women, it shouldn't matter. No one should be exempted from being respectful and acting like a team player.

*Let's do better.*

This experience taught me that leadership is about respect and teamwork. In the real world, true leadership means standing up for what's right, even when it's uncomfortable. It's about creating an environment where everyone feels valued and respected, regardless of gender or background.

Leadership starts with small actions—being ready, taking the first step, and setting an example. When leaders tolerate bad behavior, they send a message that such conduct is acceptable. But by addressing these issues head-on, we can build a more inclusive and supportive workplace.

By sharing this story, I hope to inspire others to take a stand and promote a culture where everyone is treated equally. Leadership is not just about achieving personal success, but about uplifting others and fostering an environment where everyone can thrive.

So, let's commit to doing better. Let's lead with integrity, respect, and a genuine desire to make a difference. Together, we can create workplaces where everyone feels valued and empowered to reach their full potential.

*You see successful women around, dominating their industries and inspiring millions! What you don't see is their mindset.*

It's not hard rising to the top, it really isn't. All you need is the right mindset, and I hope you switch today!

## You are Unique

Absolutely, recognizing your uniqueness is crucial. It's about understanding that your life experiences, skills, and talents combine in a way that is entirely your own. This understanding empowers you to embrace your strengths and confidently contribute to the world around you.

When you acknowledge your uniqueness, you begin to value your own perspectives and abilities more deeply. This self-awareness helps you overcome doubts and insecurities that may hold you back. Instead of trying to conform to others' expectations or comparing yourself unfavorably to them, you celebrate what makes you distinct.

Leadership often stems from this confidence in one's unique abilities. A leader who embraces their individuality can inspire others to do the same. By showing authenticity and conviction in who you are, you not only lead by example but also encourage others to recognize and cultivate their own strengths.

So, yes, leaders are indeed confident. They understand and appreciate their uniqueness, which allows them to lead with authenticity and make a meaningful impact in their own way.

### *You are Worth it*

Believing in the ideas and ambitions that resonate within you is crucial to pursuing your dreams. Those aspirations are not random; they reflect your unique passions, talents, and potential. Trusting in yourself and your abilities is key to overcoming self-doubt and seizing opportunities that align with your goals.

When you recognize that opportunities come into your life for a reason, it empowers you to take action. Each opportunity is a chance to move closer to your dreams, to learn, grow, and ultimately achieve what you envision. By embracing these opportunities with courage and determination, you pave the way for turning your dreams into reality.

Remember, self-belief is fundamental. It's about acknowledging your worthiness of your dreams and goals, and understanding that you have what it takes to pursue them. As you push past doubts and seize every chance that comes your way, you're actively creating the path toward fulfilling your ambitions.

So, embrace your dreams, trust in yourself, and take bold steps forward. The journey may have challenges, but your belief in your potential will guide you toward achieving what you set out to accomplish.

### *Here's an Advice*

Sharing your knowledge is incredibly powerful and beneficial for both the giver and the receiver. When you freely share your insights, tips, and experiences, you not only contribute to the growth and success of others but also enhance your own credibility and reputation.

Gatekeeping knowledge, on the other hand, creates unnecessary barriers and fosters a culture of exclusivity. It limits the potential for collaboration and mutual learning. By hoarding information, individuals miss out on opportunities to build meaningful connections and contribute to a community of shared learning and development.

Think about the times when you've received valuable advice or guidance from someone. It likely made a significant impact on your journey and helped you navigate challenges more effectively. By sharing your own knowledge and experiences, you have the potential to positively influence others in a similar way.

Moreover, sharing knowledge often leads to unexpected benefits. When you generously offer your expertise, you create goodwill and open doors for new opportunities, collaborations, and friendships. Your willingness to contribute to the success of others fosters a supportive environment where everyone can thrive.

In summary, embracing a mindset of sharing rather than gatekeeping enriches not only your own experience but also the broader community. It promotes openness, collaboration, and continuous learning, ultimately benefiting everyone involved. So, don't hesitate to share what you know—your insights could make a profound difference in someone else's journey.

### *Let's grow as A Community*

The concept of competition can often overshadow the power of collaboration and community. When we recognize and celebrate each person's unique goals and journeys, we shift towards a more supportive and empowering environment.

Viewing others not as competitors but as members of a community allows us to leverage our collective strengths and experiences. Each individual brings something valuable to the table, and when we uplift each other, everyone benefits. Collaboration fosters innovation, shared learning, and a sense of belonging that propels everyone forward.

The idea of "women-against-women" or any form of divisive competition is indeed outdated. Instead, embracing a mindset where we actively support and encourage each other leads to greater success and fulfilment. When one person succeeds, they can pave the way for others, creating a ripple effect of empowerment.

Helping others achieve their goals not only feels fulfilling but also contributes to a more inclusive and supportive culture. It's about recognizing that our collective achievements are strengthened when we work together. By sharing resources, knowledge, and opportunities, we build a stronger network where everyone has the potential to thrive.

In essence, shifting from a competitive mindset to one of community and collaboration opens doors to new possibilities. It promotes a culture where everyone's achievements are celebrated, and challenges are faced together. This approach not only enhances individual success but also fosters a more connected and supportive society overall.

### *I'm more than enough*

Firstly, the abundance mindset emphasizes that there is more than enough success, wealth, and recognition to go around for everyone. When you shift your perspective from scarcity to abundance, you open yourself up to new opportunities and possibilities. This mindset encourages generosity, collaboration, and a positive outlook on achieving goals.

Believing in abundance allows you to see opportunities where others might see competition or limitations. It fosters a sense of empowerment and reduces stress associated with feeling like you have to constantly fight for your share. Embracing abundance can lead to a more fulfilling and satisfying journey toward success.

Secondly, the importance of diversity in leadership cannot be overstated. Integrating diverse perspectives, including those of women, enriches decision-making processes and enhances innovation within organizations. Women bring unique strengths such as empathy, adaptability, and collaborative problem-solving skills, which are increasingly valued in today's dynamic business landscape.

Despite the proven benefits of diverse leadership teams, there remains a significant gap in gender representation at senior levels. Addressing this gap isn't just about equality; it's about maximizing business potential. Companies with diverse leadership teams tend to perform better financially, innovate more effectively, and attract top talent.

By advocating for more women in leadership roles, we're not only promoting fairness but also tapping into a valuable pool of talent and perspectives that can drive organizational success. It's about creating inclusive environments where everyone can thrive and contribute their best.

In conclusion, embracing an abundance mindset and promoting diversity in leadership are interconnected principles that can lead to greater personal and organizational success. By believing in abundance and supporting diverse leadership, we can create stronger, more innovative, and more inclusive businesses and communities.

*So, how do we close this gap?*

The answer begins with us. We need to create and nurture cultures that not only welcome diversity but actively champion it. Implementing mentorship programs, offering flexible working arrangements, and supporting initiatives that elevate women are essential steps. However, these initiatives must be more than just checkboxes.

Mentorship programs only work when they result in tangible promotions for participants. It's crucial to ensure that women who go through these programs see real advancement in their careers. Flexible working arrangements should not be used as an excuse to penalize employees at the end of the year by citing the flexibility provided. Instead, these arrangements should genuinely support work-life balance without negative repercussions.

Supporting initiatives should not exist merely for appearances. It's vital to track and publicize the results—how many women have been promoted through these initiatives? How their contributions have impacted the company? What changes have been made to support their growth? Transparency in these outcomes builds trust and shows a genuine commitment to diversity.

By promoting women from mentorship programs, ensuring flexible work policies are fair and supportive, and demonstrating real results from diversity initiatives, businesses can close the gender gap in leadership. This approach drives innovation and success across the organization.

Let's not passively wait for change. Let's be the catalyst of that change. Support and champion the women in your network. Advocate for their advancement and celebrate their successes. By taking these actions, we can collectively redefine the face of leadership and unlock the full potential of our businesses.

- **Leadership is a mindset**, not just a position or title. It's more about action than theory, and it requires a strong internal drive.
- **Not everyone is suited for leadership**. Some people prefer stability and routine over the risks and challenges of leadership roles.
- **Leadership demands stepping out of comfort zones.** It involves taking risks and can sometimes mean facing fears of failure or attention.
- **The desire to lead comes from within.** It's like a fire that compels you to take action and lead the way.
- **Respect individual differences in ambition.** Not everyone has the desire to climb the corporate ladder, and that's perfectly acceptable.

I recall a conversation with a colleague during lunch, where I brought up our pay equity as women. Expecting her to share my concerns, I was surprised when she laughed it off. She said, "Hey listen, as long as we get our salary and manage our work-life balance, it's enough. We don't need to rule the world, right?" At that moment, I realized the importance of surrounding myself with people who match my level of ambition. Associating with those who are content with less can pull you down and make you settle for less than you deserve. That interaction, when I was 28, felt like a conversation with someone who had seen all they wanted in life and was ready to just coast along.

## Leading with Respect

Leadership is like discovering your unique voice in a group. To me, leading means having the courage to speak up for yourself. If you can't do that for you, how can you do it for others? It all begins with believing in yourself and staying true to what you stand for.

Think of the business world as a game where nobody is solely your friend or foe—it's really You versus You. Leadership here isn't just about the fancy title on your door; it's all about what you do and the values you believe in. Each day brings a fresh challenge, a chance to show that leadership means actually making a real impact, not just doing a job.

Many think all managers are leaders, but not all leaders have titles. In truth, real leadership goes beyond titles, fueled by passion and empathy—qualities not always found in the competitive corporate world.

Think about this: some leaders don't go after titles, but they still lead. They inspire, motivate, and make change happen. Sure, having a title can be powerful. It gives you the freedom to shake things up, adjust, tweak, and make a difference. Leadership with title, in this way, is about using your power to create real change—a freedom that also brings huge responsibilities.

As you journey on, whether you aim for a title or just want to lead change, remember that your leadership should show who you truly are. It's about being the person who isn't afraid to stand out, speak up, and guide the way when others hesitate.

## Expanding Through Leadership Skills

Why consider developing your leadership skills? What if you viewed these skills not just as tools for career advancement but as essential elements for a richer, more effective life?

Leadership training enhances your communication skills, enabling you to express your ideas and feelings more clearly. This skill is crucial not only in professional settings where clarity can drive success but also at home, where effective communication can strengthen relationships and resolve conflicts.

Problem-solving and decision-making are also key benefits of leadership development. These skills allow you to address issues creatively and make choices confidently. Whether you're dealing with a project at work or planning a family event, the ability to assess situations and make sound decisions quickly is invaluable.

Understanding people and their behaviors is another significant advantage. This insight can transform your interactions and help you build more meaningful connections. At work, it enables you to motivate and inspire your team. In personal settings, it helps you understand friends and family better, leading to more harmonious relationships.

Emphasizing these skills is crucial as they prepare you for professional roles and a fulfilling and effective life. They equip you with the qualities necessary to lead—with or without a title.

By investing in your leadership capabilities, you're not just preparing to take on more significant challenges; you're gearing up to lead a more accomplished, satisfying life. *Isn't that worth considering?*

*Cultivating a Positive Corporate Culture Through Leadership*

Strong leadership transforms corporate culture and elevates employee engagement by creating an environment where employees feel valued and understood. Leaders who prioritize a positive culture set the stage for meaningful work, clear goals, and ample opportunities for growth and development.

Leaders are the architects of this environment. The structures and systems they implement are not just administrative; they are the scaffolding that supports and guides desired behaviors. What kind of behaviors are encouraged in your company? How are these behaviors reinforced by the actions and examples set by those at the top?

Consider the power of practice in leadership. It's one thing to propose a set of values or principles—it's another to embody them daily. This alignment between saying and doing is critical. When leaders consistently demonstrate the values they preach, they embed these principles deeply within the corporate culture.

This is important because employees pay close attention. They notice when leaders "walk the walk" and when they merely "*talk the talk.*" When leadership practices what they preach, it doesn't just set a standard—it inspires. Employees become more engaged, not just with their tasks but with the mission of the organization as a whole. They are more likely to feel satisfied with their work, motivated to give their best, and invested in the long-term success of the company.

In a competitive landscape where a company's culture can mean the difference between retaining top talent or facing a shortage, leaders must be aware of their daily impact on the workplace, intentional or not.

- **Leadership is a choice:** Every individual has the option to lead or to wait for others to lead. The decision to act is what sets leaders apart.
- **Leadership drives change:** Stagnation is detrimental. Without the drive for continual improvement and change, organizations risk falling behind. Effective leaders are agents of change.
- **Leadership is universal:** Everyone has the potential to lead within their own areas. The belief that only those at the top can lead is a myth that limits potential and stifles innovation.
- **Leadership can be developed:** It grows best in supportive, small-group environments where individuals can practice, reflect, and encourage one another. Passion and perseverance are key to developing leadership skills.
- **Leadership nurtures courage:** In small groups, aspiring leaders find the safety to express themselves and challenge the status quo, which cultivates the courage needed to lead.

## Leadership at Every Level: Why It's a Game-Changer

*Think leadership is only for the top brass?* Think again! Leadership isn't a privilege reserved for the few at the top; it's essential for everyone, at every rung of the ladder. *Why?* Because nurturing leadership skills across the board breeds a high-performance culture that's agile, innovative, and downright unstoppable.

Climbing to the top may seem straightforward, but making your mark and staying there is the real challenge. It's more than just hard work and dedication; it's about mastering a robust set of skills that keep you one step ahead.

Consider the idea of leading by example. It is simple yet powerful. Want a hardworking and productive team? Show them how it is done. Expect honesty and integrity? Be the mirror reflecting those values every day. This is not just about setting standards; it is about embedding these qualities into the team.

Take a page from my early career: I worked closely with a Global Delivery Head who was the epitome of leadership. He treated everyone respectfully and never let his power go to his head. His humility and open-door policy weren't just for show—He treated everyone equally and remained easily approachable, even to newcomers. He taught me that a true leader doesn't just lead; they make you feel good about being part of the team.

Inspired by him, I set out to forge my style. Leading with empathy but setting clear boundaries—it's crucial, especially when you're steering a large team. It helps prevent burnout and keeps you focused. Defining these mental boundaries ensures you lead effectively without getting overwhelmed.

So, whether you're just starting or you're already leading teams, remember: that leadership is about influence, not authority. It's about making an impact at every level, and it's definitely about making people feel valued and motivated. That's how you create a culture where everyone is geared up to excel, not just comply.

## Accepting Diversity and Inclusion in Leadership

Great leaders know they're not alone; they are part of a community that thrives on collective effort and shared victories. This belief that "*We achieve more together than alone*" is fundamental to successful leadership.

Leaders who excel encourage creativity and innovation by making genuine connections with their team members. They invest time to understand each individual's strengths and weaknesses, which helps them place the right person in the right role, boosting both efficiency and productivity. Moreover, a leader's ability to learn from their team is crucial. Surrounding oneself with a diverse group of smart individuals is not just useful; it's essential. These team members contribute a variety of ideas and feedback, which drives the team's success and helps everyone, including the leaders, to enhance their skills and grow both personally and professionally.

Today's corporate leadership space shows a significant imbalance—90% men and less than 10% women in top positions. Despite policies reserving 30% of leadership roles for women, this goal often remains unmet. The common explanation is the lack of suitable internal or external candidates, indicating a failure to cultivate or attract diverse talent.

My personal experience sheds light on the consequences of ignoring diversity. In a previous role, women were routinely left out of crucial discussions yet were expected to carry out tasks without being fully informed. When I stood up to highlight this discrepancy, it led to targeted attempts by the leadership to push me out, favoring those who upheld the status quo. This kind of leadership not only suppresses innovation but also creates a toxic environment that drives away competent, hard-working employees. This allows less capable individuals to advance, further degrading the quality of leadership and effectiveness which is the case mostly.

Diversity is not merely a buzzword; it's the foundation of a robust and innovative workplace. True innovation arises from the confluence of diverse perspectives, which challenge each other and push the limits of what's possible.

Leaders who prioritize diversity and inclusion not only create a healthier, more vibrant organizational culture but also ensure that their teams are well-equipped to navigate the complexities of a global market. This approach makes organizations stronger and more competitive.

## The Power of Confidence in Leadership

Developing self-confidence every day is crucial, especially when surrounded by people who may lack ambition or clear goals. This practice helps to maintain your focus and drive, reinforcing your belief in your own capabilities.

It's essential to remain open to learning from others, not just imparting knowledge. No leader knows everything, and recognizing this can dramatically enhance your leadership by fostering a culture of continuous learning and humility.

True confidence comes from within, and so does a leadership mindset. It's important to remind yourself regularly of your worth, potential, and value—concepts that can sometimes feel distant, especially when faced with the endless comparisons drawn on platforms like social media. Keeping inspirational quotes handy can be a powerful tool. As Johann Wolfgang von Goethe said, *"As soon as you trust yourself, you will know how to live."* This suggests that constantly trying to prove yourself can sometimes do more harm than good.

Remember, striving for something seemingly better can sometimes lead to losing what was good to begin with. It's crucial not to underestimate the value of what you currently have.

Here are some practices that have been instrumental in my growth as a leader:

- Keep an open mind to different opinions.
- Maintain a consistently positive outlook on life.
- Practice patience, compassion, and empathy.
- Develop strong emotional intelligence.
- Emit a positive energy that attracts like-minded individuals.
- Allow others the space to express their thoughts and complete their stories.
- Be someone people can rely on, not just in critical moments but always.

- Encourage others to shine and genuinely celebrate their successes.
- Be willing to acknowledge mistakes—yours and others—and learn from them.
- Prioritize listening over speaking; hearing others out is often more important than being heard.

## Initiative to Influence

I didn't become a leader by following someone else's example. Instead, I learned from watching leaders I didn't want to be like, and from situations I hoped to avoid.

I've always believed that you can be kind and humble and still stand up for yourself and your team when needed. This belief was tested before I officially became a leader. Back then, I wasn't a manager by title, but I was doing everything a manager would do.

There was a big project that needed to be done—a program that had to be delivered to the whole organization in just three months. It was tough because I didn't have a title, and sometimes people didn't take me seriously. Some even tried to discourage me, asking why I bothered since management didn't see any value in it.

But I was passionate about making it happen, so I kept going. It was hard, though, and there came a point when I felt like I might break down. I was trying to be authentic and honest, but not everyone was supportive.

That's when I went to the center head and told him I needed a title to get things done. He asked me, *"How will that make a difference?"* I explained that a title would give me the authority to be taken seriously, just like it did for him. He listened and promised that if I could pull off the program with all these challenges, he would make sure I got that title.

This conversation changed how I approached things. I started to focus on talking to people differently and being assertive. I got better at showing my team what was in it for them and got their buy-in. Things started to move smoother after that.

The program was a success because I made everyone feel like they owned it. I learned that leadership isn't about just leading; it's about knowing when to step back and let others lead, supporting them when they need it. From this program, I helped develop two new leaders who are now doing great in their careers.

*Influence Without a Title*

*How do you tell if someone is a successful leader?*

It's not always about hitting specific targets or metrics. Sometimes, the true measure of leadership is found in the lessons learned from each experience, not just the outcomes. A leader's success can be gauged by their ability to turn even failures into insights that refine their next efforts.

Leadership often grows through action more than through reading about it. It's about putting yourself out there, trying new things, and seeing what you can learn from them. For example, think about a simple act like celebrating a colleague's birthday. Instead of just saying "Happy birthday," imagine organizing the whole team to sing together. Most people will join in because it's fun and they know each other.

Now, take it a step further: what if you tried to get a group of strangers on a bus to sing *"Happy Birthday" for someone?* This is more challenging because these people don't know each other. Yet, if you can pull it off, it teaches you about leadership in a deeper way. It shows you how to inspire a group of strangers to come together for a single moment of joy.

This kind of experiment doesn't just benefit others; it helps you develop crucial leadership qualities like boldness, courage, and the ability to engage others. It's about presenting an idea so appealingly that people feel eager to join in, even if there's no obvious reward or reason. This teaches you to be the face of an initiative, to manage and motivate, and to create a positive impact through collaborative effort.

## Era of Change

We find ourselves in an era where sometimes it feels like intelligent discourse is muted to avoid offending. Ever found yourself in such a situation? It's a curious time to be a leader or an aspiring one.

Just like you can't learn to drive without getting behind the wheel, or become a photographer without snapping photos, you can't truly learn leadership from a textbook. You learn by doing—by speaking in public, by leading a team, by handling real challenges.

The key is to believe in yourself and take the first step. The perfect time will never just appear; you have to make it. Waiting around for the ideal moment might mean you'll wait forever.

## Exploring the Leadership Headstand Technique

Let's talk about a unique concept: the Leadership Headstand technique. It's not just a physical inversion—

it's a metaphor for turning your approach to problems upside down.

Performing a headstand, literally or figuratively, can shift your perspective dramatically. It pushes you to look at situations from a different angle and can lead to surprising breakthroughs.

This technique involves brainstorming by reversing the meaning of your original questions. It's about challenging your usual way of thinking and uncovering creative, alternative solutions.

How does it work? Start by asking a positive question, then flip it to its negative counterpart.

For instance:

- *Positive question: How can I motivate my team?*
- *Negative version: How can I demotivate my team?*

From the negative, you generate ideas such as not responding to requests for help, blaming the team for delays, or failing to set clear goals. These actions form a 'Not-to-do list' which, when reversed, guides you toward motivating your team effectively.

By deliberately considering what could demotivate your team, you become more aware of the actions you should avoid and the ones that truly inspire and drive your team forward.

Leadership is not just about guiding others; it's about innovative thinking and finding solutions that defy the ordinary. The Headstand technique is just one way to enhance your creative problem-solving skills and ensure you're supporting your team in the most effective ways possible.

*"Believe in yourself and all that you are.
Know that there is something inside you
that is greater than any obstacle."*

– Christian D. Larson

CHAPTER 2

# AWAKEN YOUR INNER STRENGTHS

## *Finding the Strength, You Didn't Know You Had*

Your greatest test often comes when you have to handle people who mishandle you. One day, I decided to pursue a PMP certification, a prestigious milestone in project management. Back in the early 2000s, being PMP certified was a big deal, and I was determined to be among the first 4,000 people in the world to achieve it.

I attended a five-day classroom training and eagerly scheduled my exam for December 18th. Coincidentally, I was also expecting a baby in December and had planned to become PMP-certified while my baby was still inside me. But life had other plans.

I delivered my son on December 12th. Naturally, my mom was against the idea of me stepping out of the house to take an exam right after childbirth. I didn't have the heart to go against her advice, so I postponed my PMP exam March.

I soon realized I was already part of a complex project—my baby! My sleep schedule, eating habits, body, and priorities all changed. Being a new mom and adapting to my son's routine was challenging and exhausting. I knew I would have to postpone my exam again, and eventually, I opted for a refund, deciding to wait until I was ready mentally and physically.

I returned to work after maternity leave, focusing on my team and projects. Yet, in the back of my mind, I still wanted to crack the PMP exam. After two years, I made up my mind, quit my job, and dedicated myself to achieving my certification. I took care of my son during the day and studied at night, avoiding distractions. Within three months, I passed my PMP exam with flying colors!

*I was over the moon, even though I didn't had a job lined up.*

Passion is the driving force behind all great achievements. It fuels our ambitions and propels us toward our goals. It's that internal fire that motivates us to strive for success, even when external circumstances seem daunting or challenging.

In my journey to become PMP certified, it wasn't external pressure or societal expectations that pushed me to succeed—it was an internal drive. Despite the challenges I faced as a new mother and the setbacks along the way, it was my passion and determination that kept me focused on my goal.

Passion provides the energy needed to overcome obstacles and adapt to changing circumstances. It's the key to turning dreams into reality because it keeps us moving forward, even when the going gets tough. The real pressure comes from within, and it's this internal pressure that keeps us striving to be our best selves.

*Passion is our energy. It's the fire that drives us to achieve anything. It's never about external pressure, but always about the push from within.*

*So, did my story inspire you enough to take your next big step?*

What does "inner strengths" mean to you? These are the qualities and traits within you that help you push forward, especially when climbing the corporate ladder. They're the resilience, courage, and determination that keep you going, even when things get tough. Cultivating these strengths is crucial for anyone aiming to succeed in their career.

Here's how you can nurture and awaken your inner strengths every single day:

1. **Revisit Your Vision Daily, and Take Action:** It's important to keep your goals in mind, but also to take the necessary steps towards achieving them. Simply dreaming isn't enough; you need to pair your vision with action.
2. **Accept Failure as Part of the Process, and Keep Trying:** Everyone encounters setbacks, but it's crucial not to give up easily. Learn from failures and use them as stepping stones to improve and grow.
3. **Approach Problems from All Sides, and Make Wise Decisions:** Take time to look at challenges from different angles before deciding on a course of action. This thoughtful approach will help you make informed decisions.
4. **Put Yourself in Challenging Situations, and Learn and Lead:** Stepping out of your comfort zone can be intimidating, but it's where you grow the most. Embrace challenges as opportunities to learn and lead.
5. **Always Be in Motion: Provide Value, and Ensure You're Valued Too:** Contribute to your team and

organization, but also make sure that your efforts are recognized and appreciated.

6. **Use Networks to Build Connections, and Help Them Grow Too:** Networking is vital for building business relationships. It's also important to help others grow, creating mutually beneficial connections.

*Focus on Things That People Can't Take Away from You*

As you climb the Leadership ladder, it's important to focus on things that can't be taken away from you—qualities that truly matter and define who you are. These include:

- **Character:** The essence of who you are and how you treat others. It's built over time and is a true reflection of your values and principles.
- **Mindset:** Your outlook on life and work. A positive, growth-oriented mindset helps you tackle challenges and pursue opportunities.
- **Values:** The beliefs that guide your decisions and actions. Staying true to your values gives you a strong foundation, especially in challenging times.
- **Integrity:** The consistency of your actions and values. Maintaining your integrity earns you respect and trust, both professionally and personally.
- **Discipline:** The ability to stay focused and work towards your goals, even when it's tough. Discipline helps you achieve what you set out to do.

- **Your Well-Being:** Taking care of your physical and mental health ensures you have the energy and resilience to face whatever comes your way.

## Finding and Revealing Inner Strengths

There are moments in life that test our inner strengths and reveal what we're truly capable of. One of the best ways to uncover these moments is to celebrate our small wins, as they often lead to bigger victories.

You should step out of your comfort zone only when being in that zone becomes uncomfortable. Let me explain.

I worked from home for more than a decade. Life seemed comfortable—I had a secure job, a good salary, and all the comforts I needed. But as time went on, I started feeling mentally trapped and uncomfortable, even though I was physically secure. So, I decided to quit my job.

I made this choice to move to a place that was more comfortable mentally, even if it meant facing some physical discomfort, like driving to work almost every day. Many of my former colleagues, who also worked from home full-time, didn't share my feelings. They were happy and content with what they had, which is absolutely fine. If they had quit their jobs, their lives would have become more uncomfortable. They had no goals, and they were happy with what they had.

If you have a comfortable life, don't take it for granted. And don't leave this zone thinking a new life will be naturally better. You should only leave your comfort zone when it becomes uncomfortable for you.

## Feedbacks change your mindset

Feedback from colleagues, mentors, or coaches can be incredibly valuable in helping us recognize our strengths. One of the most impactful feedback moments in my career came on my last working day at my first corporate job.

I approached a senior colleague and asked him to share three good things and three bad things about me. He smiled and said, "You're a passionate professional. Everyone admires you for your perfection and the way you manage the team with ease."

Hearing this made me feel proud, but when it came to the bad things, he hesitated. Finally, he said, "I don't have three bad things, but I have one: Don't expect everyone to be perfect like you."

That feedback stayed with me for a long time. Taking it positively helped me discover more about myself. Feedback like this can be an eye-opener. It reminds us that while it's great to strive for perfection, it's also important to recognize that not everyone shares the same standards or approach.

Taking feedback regularly from colleagues, managers, parents, and even children helps you become a better person. It's crucial to know yourself and identify your own red flags and toxic traits.

We've all heard the term "red flag" used to describe someone else. But how often do we consider that we might be the red flag in someone else's life? Everyone has flaws, and it's important to conduct regular self-checks to ensure we're being our best selves.

Constructive feedback helps us see our blind spots and improve on areas we might not have realized needed attention. It's not about being perfect, but about continuously learning and growing.

## Signs You Might Be a Red Flag

After reflecting on the impact of feedback, let's look at some signs that might indicate if you're a red flag. Recognizing these traits can help you become your best self.

- **You Lack Empathy:** Empathy is about understanding and sharing the feelings of others. If you struggle with empathy, you might come across as uncaring or cold, which can hurt your relationships. Working on empathy helps you connect with others and build stronger bonds.
- **You're Not Willing to Work on Yourself:** Personal development is key to overcoming challenges and becoming a better person. By refusing to change or grow, you risk becoming stagnant and disconnected from those around you.
- **You're Too Self-Centered:** Self-love is important, but being self-centered is different. When you're self-centered, you focus only on your needs and ignore the needs of others. This attitude can damage relationships and prevent you from being a supportive friend or partner.
- **You Can't Handle Rejection:** Rejections are a part of life. Whether it's in relationships, jobs, or personal goals, not everything will go your

way. Learning to accept rejection and using it as a stepping stone to success is crucial.

- **You Do the Bare Minimum:** Doing just enough to get by might seem fine at first, but it often leads to missed opportunities and stagnant growth. To achieve anything meaningful, you need to put in effort and go beyond the minimum.
- **You're Not a Good Listener:** Listening is a super skill for life. It's not just about hearing words; it's about understanding and being present for others. If you're not a good listener, you might miss out on important information or fail to support the people you care about.

No matter how great we think we are at anything, there is always someone better than us. Always! So, find them, follow them, read or listen to their work, engage with them, collaborate with them, and learn from them. Stay curious and keep learning.

## Nurturing and Developing Your Strengths

What practices or habits have you found effective in nurturing and developing your strengths?

One valuable approach is recognizing that smart work is a byproduct of hard work, not the other way around. So, when someone says, *"I don't work hard, I work smart,"* I often wonder who they're trying to fool.

All the billionaires out there—those who have achieved remarkable success—work for themselves, not for someone else. This isn't to say you have to start your own business, but it's crucial to invest in yourself.

It's important not to fall for the stereotype of working smart without working hard. You might later regret it. In the beginning, regardless of what you do, you have to put in the hard work to make an impact. Working hard is the initial task while working smart is the reward you earn afterward.

Remember, hard work can beat smart work if smart work doesn't put in the effort.

Therefore, smart work is often a result of hard work. You need to complete the task before you can enjoy the reward.

## Balancing Strengths and Weaknesses

When it comes to dealing with challenges and personal growth, I've noticed that people often fall into one of two categories:

**Complainers:** These folks seem to focus on everything wrong. They often blame others or situations for their shortcomings, feeling like external factors are holding them back from achieving their goals.

**Believers:** These people, on the other hand, see challenges as opportunities. They believe that every person they meet and every experience they have can help them move closer to their goals. They see failures as chances to learn and improve.

In my experience, adopting the mindset of a Believer helps you balance focusing on your strengths while also addressing your weaknesses.

To start, it helps to recognize what you're good at. For example, I've found that when I focus on my strengths, like communication or problem-solving, I feel more confident and motivated. It's not about ignoring your weaknesses, but rather about using your strengths as a foundation to build upon.

At the same time, it's important to address areas where you need improvement. For example, I've had to work on being more patient. Instead of seeing my weaknesses as obstacles, I've tried to view it as an opportunity to learn and grow. Guess writing this book has helped to an extent.

- **Striking a Balance**

Balancing both strengths and weaknesses isn't always easy, but it's worth the effort. I've found that by focusing on what I'm good at while also being mindful of areas for improvement, I become more resilient and better prepared for challenges. It's all about having the right mindset—one that encourages you to see both strengths and weaknesses as parts of a larger journey.

## Leveraging Inner Strengths to Overcome Workplace Challenges

*"If opportunity doesn't knock, build a door."* This quote captures the essence of taking charge of your destiny. In the workplace, understanding and leveraging your inner strengths can be the key to creating your own opportunities.

You can create these opportunities simply by putting yourself out there. Sometimes, things take longer than expected, but it's important to plant the seeds and give them time to sprout. In my experience, being proactive and embracing challenges has often led to unexpected and rewarding outcomes.

Being your own cheerleader is crucial. It's easy to get caught up in self-doubt or to focus on external validation, but the truth is, no one can cheer you on better than yourself. By believing in your abilities and strengths, you set the stage for success. At the same time, it's important to cheer for others and help them grow as well. This creates a positive and supportive environment where everyone can thrive.

It's also important to be unapologetic about what you want. By understanding your strengths and focusing on your goals, you can confidently pursue what matters most to you. This clarity and determination can help you navigate workplace challenges with a clear sense of purpose.

Continue to believe and work consistently, keeping an open mind, and you'll see magical things happen! The best project you'll ever work on is yourself. Investing in your personal development and growth will give you the greatest return on investment, whether it's in better relationships, better results, or better finances.

By focusing on leveraging your inner strengths, you can approach workplace challenges with a sense of confidence and resilience, knowing that you're building a strong foundation for long-term success.

## Strengths and Resilience

Inner strengths play a crucial role in building resilience. They've certainly helped me bounce back from setbacks. One of the key things I've learned is not to shy away from being an inspiration or hearing that you are an inspiration to others.

Being an inspiration means you've made a difference—you've lived a life that's useful, impactful, and compassionate. It's about being there for others and showing them that it's possible to overcome challenges and achieve great things.

To inspire others is to be useful to them, to honor them, and to have compassion for them. These qualities come from inner strengths like empathy, kindness, and determination. When we face setbacks, these strengths help us stay grounded, see the bigger picture, and keep moving forward.

Next time you're inspired by someone, don't hesitate to tell them. It means a lot to hear that you've made a positive impact on someone's life. Similarly, when people tell you that you're an inspiration, embrace it. It's a reminder that your inner strengths are shining through, even in tough times.

Understanding and nurturing these strengths allows you to face challenges with confidence and bounce back from difficulties with grace. It's a powerful way to lead and live, making the world a better place one step at a time.

## Building a Strong Team by Leveraging Strengths

As a leader, one of the most rewarding things you can do is help your team members identify and play to their strengths. By doing this, you create a team so strong that, as the saying goes, anyone who sees it doesn't know who the leader is.

I know some managers might feel threatened by this idea, fearing that their team's success might overshadow their own. But in reality, when you help your team members shine, you have more time and space to focus on bigger and better things.

Helping your team identify their strengths starts with understanding each person's unique talents and abilities. I've found that having regular one-on-one conversations, asking questions, and really listening to what your team members enjoy and excel at can reveal a lot about their strengths.

Encouraging team members to take on new challenges and explore different roles also helps them discover their strengths. For example, I once encouraged a team member to lead a project even though she was hesitant. It turned out to be a great opportunity for her to showcase her organizational skills and creativity, which boosted her confidence and brought a fresh perspective to the team.

Building a supportive environment where team members feel comfortable sharing their ideas and trying new things is key. When people feel valued and trusted, they're more likely to step up and use their strengths effectively.

By cultivating an environment where everyone is encouraged to excel, you create a team that thrives on collaboration and mutual respect. It's not about individual titles or roles but about building a cohesive unit where everyone's strengths contribute to the collective success.

Ultimately, as a leader, helping your team members identify and leverage their strengths not only benefits them but also makes the team stronger and more resilient as a whole. It's a win-win situation that leads to a happier, more productive workplace.

## Discovering Your Inner Strengths

If you feel like you haven't discovered your inner strengths yet, don't worry—everyone goes through this phase. The key is to remember that making right and wrong decisions is a natural part of life.

When you're right, take the lead. When you're wrong, learn from it. Learning and leading are like two eyes in the game of leadership. By listening to your heart and staying ahead, you can gradually uncover your unique strengths.

Discipline is crucial for discovering anything in this world, whether it's your inner strengths or external goals.

It's often said that discipline is doing what needs to be done, even when you don't want to do it. This means sticking to your goals and pushing through even when it's tough or uncomfortable.

To discover your strengths, start by exploring what excites you or where you naturally excel. Trying new things, reflecting on your experiences, and being open to feedback can all help you uncover what you're good at and what brings you joy.

It's also important to be patient with yourself. Strengths don't always reveal themselves overnight. Sometimes, they emerge when you least expect them, especially when you're focused on learning and growing.

By staying disciplined, exploring new opportunities, and being open to both leading and learning, you'll eventually discover your inner strengths. And once you do, you'll be well on your way to achieving great things.

### *Discipline is Easy! You Just Don't Know These Secrets* ☺

- **Find Your Why:** Connecting every task to a deeper purpose helps make discipline easier. When you have a strong "why" behind what you do, it becomes easier to stay motivated and focused, even when things get tough.
- **Routine is Key**: Setting a daily routine that aligns with your goals can make a big difference. When you have a structured plan for each day, it helps you stay on track and make consistent progress toward your objectives.
- **Mindset Matters**: Seeing discipline as an opportunity, not as a burden, can transform your approach. By viewing discipline as a chance to grow and improve, you can approach tasks with a positive attitude and stay motivated.
- **Celebrate Small Wins**: Small wins lead to bigger wins. Celebrating your achievements, no matter how small keeps your momentum alive and reminds you of the progress you're making.

- **Visualize**: Visualization is like mentally preparing for reality. By picturing yourself achieving your goals and overcoming challenges, you set yourself up for success and build confidence in your ability to stay disciplined.
- **Circle Back**: Regularly reviewing your progress and adjusting if needed helps you stay on course. By checking in with yourself and making changes as necessary, you ensure that you're always moving toward your goals.

## Choose Your Circle Wisely

One of the most important things in life is to choose your circle wisely. The wrong people won't help you progress, but the right people can be a source of inspiration, support, motivation, respect, and trust.

If you can't find such people, be that person for yourself. By being a positive influence, you can inspire others to do the same.

Surrounding yourself with people who uplift you and align with your goals and values can make a world of difference. It's about creating a circle where everyone grows together, each person inspiring and helping the other to be the best version of themselves.

If you can't find such people, *be that person for yourself.*

Eventually, *you will inspire others to be one too!*

*"Leadership is not about the role you're given; it's about what we do with that role."*

– Kavitha Ramakrishnappa

CHAPTER 3

# UNPACKING THE ROLES

One common misconception in the corporate world is that managers are always the problem.

I was having lunch with a colleague who started venting about his manager. He felt that his manager was always finding faults in his work and treating him badly. He was clearly frustrated and unhappy.

I listened to him without interrupting, and when he finished, I asked if he had more complaints. He looked at me, still frustrated, and said, "Aren't these enough?"

I smiled and asked him if he had ever talked about these issues with his manager. He hadn't. I suggested, "Why don't you schedule a one-on-one meeting with your manager and speak about how you feel?" He dismissed the idea, saying, "No point & it's useless."

He didn't take my advice, and soon after, he resigned. His manager did not try to persuade him to stay, which seemed to confirm his feelings. I stayed out of it because I wasn't fully aware of all the details.

A few months later, this former colleague called me asking if there were any openings in his old team. He wanted to return because his new manager was, according to him, even worse. I gave him the same advice as before: talk to your manager about how you're feeling. Again, he was reluctant and said "No point & it's useless"

I had to be straightforward with him, "I can guide you, but if you don't value what I say, I can't help you."

He was disappointed and asked if I could talk to his ex-manager. Remembering his earlier reluctance to take action, I replied, "No point, and it's useless."

It's easy to fall into the trap of blaming managers for everything that feels wrong in our careers—from frustrations and misunderstandings to our own insecurities. However, it's important to stop and reflect on how much of this is truly due to management, and how much might be within our own control.

**Stop Blaming Managers:** It's crucial to move away from automatically saying that managers are bad or assuming they are the source of all problems. This mindset can prevent us from seeing the full picture and addressing the real issues.

**Communicate Effectively:** If you have issues or concerns at work, genuinely talk to your manager. A healthy relationship with your manager is based on open communication. It's about discussing problems directly and seeking solutions together, rather than harboring resentment or misunderstanding.

**Take Responsibility for Your Career:** Remember, while your manager can provide support and guidance, the responsibility for your career growth lies with you. Don't blame your manager or anyone else for your failures. Instead, use setbacks as learning opportunities and take proactive steps to achieve your career goals.

*Remember, your manager is not responsible of your career, but you are!*

Think of your job like a puzzle. Each piece of the puzzle represents a different task or responsibility you have. Unpacking roles is to taking a closer look at each role you interact with to see how it fits into the bigger picture of your work.

First, you lay out all the pieces. These pieces include things you do daily, like attending meetings, completing tasks, and collaborating with colleagues. Each piece has its own shape and place in the puzzle.

Some pieces fit together easily. These are the tasks you enjoy and excel at. They make sense to you, and you know exactly where they belong. Other pieces might be more challenging. They don't seem to fit right away, and you might have to try different approaches to find where they belong.

Just like some puzzle pieces have edges that connect with other pieces, you connect with your manager, your team, and your colleagues. Understanding these connections helps you see how your role fits into the larger picture of the organization.

Sometimes, you might realize that a piece is missing or doesn't fit well. Maybe you're taking on tasks that aren't really part of your main responsibilities, or you feel overwhelmed by too many pieces that don't seem to fit together. By reflecting you can identify areas that need adjustment or improvement.

This process helps you see the complete picture of your job more clearly. You understand what each piece represents and how it contributes to your work. It also helps you find ways to improve your performance and build better relationships with your colleagues.

*It's of utmost importance to understand the different parts we play in our work lives. It's about looking at our responsibilities, how we interact with others, and what we can do to improve.*

## Communication is not the Key but Keyholder

Building a good relationship with your manager is important for handling workplace challenges. Managers don't always know everything that's going on, so they need open communication to understand your perspective and help you succeed.

Start by having regular check-ins. These one-on-one meetings are a great time to talk about your progress, share concerns, and get feedback. They show your manager that you care about your work and are proactive.

Being honest is key to building trust. If you're struggling with something or if something is bothering you, speak up. Managers appreciate it when you are open and honest. It helps them understand how to support you better.

Ask for feedback often. Don't wait for annual reviews. Regularly asking for feedback shows that you want to improve and that you value your manager's opinion. This helps you stay on track and fix any issues early.

When you bring up a concern, try to also suggest a solution. This shows that you're not just complaining but thinking about how to make things better. It makes the conversation more productive and shows that you can solve problems.

Try to understand your manager's point of view. Knowing their challenges and priorities helps you communicate better and shows that you care about their perspective too. This can make your relationship stronger.

Talking openly helps solve problems at work. If there's an issue, keeping it to yourself is the worst thing you can do. Clear communication helps avoid misunderstandings that can lead to bigger problems. It makes sure everyone knows what's expected.

Communicating openly builds trust between you and your manager. Trust is the foundation of any good working relationship. It makes handling challenges easier and helps you work better together. It also encourages a team environment where people feel comfortable sharing their thoughts and ideas.

Open communication creates a positive work environment. It reduces stress, improves morale, and makes everyone feel valued and heard. Effective communication with your manager is not just about sharing your concerns but also about listening to them. It's about being honest, proactive, and ready to find solutions.

By talking openly, you can build a stronger, more trusting relationship with your manager. This is important for your career growth and for creating a positive work environment where everyone can do their best.

## Take Responsibility for Your Career

Taking charge of your career is essential. It's not true that your manager or company is responsible for your career growth, but the truth is, it is you. Your career is your journey, and you need to be in the driver's seat.

First, set clear goals. Know where you want to go and what you want to achieve. This gives you a direction and helps you make decisions that align with your aspirations. Without clear goals, it's easy to get lost or drift aimlessly.

Next, seek out opportunities for learning and growth. This could mean taking on new projects, attending workshops, or asking for additional responsibilities. Don't wait for opportunities to come to you. Go out and find them. Show that you are eager to learn and grow.

Accept setbacks as learning opportunities. Everyone faces challenges and failures, but it's how you respond to them that matters. When something goes wrong, take a step back and think about what you can learn from the experience. What could you do differently next time? How can this setback make you stronger? This mindset turns obstacles into stepping stones.

Be proactive about your development. Regularly seek feedback from your manager and colleagues. Use this feedback to improve and to track your progress. Don't be afraid to ask for help or advice. It shows that you are committed to getting better.

Take time to reflect on your achievements and areas for improvement. Celebrate your successes, no matter how small, and use them as motivation to keep pushing forward. At the same time, be honest about where you need to improve and take action to address those areas.

Network with others in your industry. Building relationships with colleagues, mentors, and other professionals can open doors to new opportunities and provide valuable support and advice. Don't underestimate the power of a strong professional network.

Stay adaptable and open to change. The business world is always evolving, and being able to adapt to new situations is a key part of career growth. Be open to new ideas and willing to adjust your plans as needed.

## Understanding and Overcoming Workplace Stereotypes

Stereotypes in the workplace can deeply affect how individuals are seen in their roles. They often limit potential and hinder true collaboration. These stereotypes create barriers that impact professional relationships and growth, making it crucial to address and overcome them.

Workplace stereotypes are subtle but powerful. They influence how colleagues interact, how opportunities are distributed, and how performance is perceived. For instance, if someone is stereotyped as not being assertive, they may be overlooked for leadership roles, even if they have the necessary skills. This can lead to frustration and hinder career growth.

Stereotypes can also damage relationships. When people make assumptions based on stereotypes, it creates a lack of trust and understanding. This can result in a divided workplace where collaboration and teamwork suffer. Recognizing and addressing these biases is essential for creating an inclusive and supportive work environment.

## Building Trust and Dismantling Stereotypes

Building trust starts with being true to yourself. When you stay true to your values and principles, people begin to respect your genuine actions and intentions. Authenticity helps dismantle stereotypes by showing your true character and abilities, beyond preconceived notions.

I remember early in my career, feeling the pressure to meet certain expectations that didn't align with who I was. Over time, I realized that staying true to myself and my values earned me more respect and trust from my colleagues. Authenticity breaks down barriers and builds genuine connections.

Stereotypes are often rooted in ignorance. By initiating open discussions and challenging misconceptions when you see them, you can help educate your peers and bring about a change in perspective. Don't be afraid to speak up and address stereotypes directly. This can help others see beyond their biases and appreciate the diversity within the team.

During a team meeting, I once heard a colleague make a stereotypical remark about another team member's capabilities. Instead of letting it slide, I gently challenged the comment and shared examples of the team member's excellent work. This opened up a discussion about the importance of judging individuals based on their actions, not stereotypes.

Making an effort to understand your colleagues' experiences and viewpoints helps reduce prejudice and build a more inclusive workplace. One of the most impactful moments in my career was when I took the time to learn about a colleague's cultural background and personal experiences. This not only deepened our working relationship but also helped me understand the unique perspectives they brought to the team.

Continuously improving your skills and consistently delivering excellent work are powerful ways to counter stereotypes about your abilities. Let your competence speak for itself. When people see your dedication and quality of work, it challenges their preconceived notions and changes their perception of you.

I faced a stereotype early on that women in my role weren't as technically proficient. Instead of letting this discourage me, I focused on honing my skills and consistently delivering high-quality work. Over time, my competence and results spoke louder than any stereotype.

Supporting colleagues when they are unfairly stereotyped strengthens individual relationships and enhances team dynamics. I once witnessed a colleague being unfairly stereotyped during a project. By standing up for them and highlighting their contributions, I helped shift the team's perception and supported a more inclusive environment.

Creating an inclusive workplace culture involves everyone. Encourage practices that promote diversity and inclusion. Celebrate the achievements of all team members and ensure that everyone has equal access to opportunities. In one of my previous roles, we started an initiative to celebrate the diverse backgrounds of our team members. This included sharing stories, hosting cultural events, and recognizing contributions from everyone. This initiative not only built a stronger sense of community but also helped to break down stereotypes.

## Accepting Authenticity Over Approval

In my career, I learned a lot about being authentic versus seeking approval. Early on, I often tried to please everyone. I would agree with others, even when I disagreed inside, just to avoid conflict or to be liked. Over time, I realized this wasn't good for anyone—not my team, not my work, and definitely not for me.

Being true to yourself is powerful. It builds trust and earns more respect than just being nice. For example, there was a project meeting where I had a different opinion. I was nervous about sharing it because it wasn't the popular view. But when I finally spoke up, it led to a better outcome. This taught me that my ideas and what I think of myself are more important than trying to get everyone's approval.

I also stopped worrying so much about what others thought of me. Focusing on being true to myself changed everything. The less I tried to get approval, the more respect I got from my peers. It felt free to realize that I didn't have to be "nice" all the time. It's okay to feel and show emotions like sadness, happiness, anger, and excitement. Expressing my true feelings, even when frustrated, led to more productive talks than just forcing a smile.

One thing I noticed was that people who always seek approval often feel the most unappreciated. But those who are just themselves—warts and all—are usually the ones who are respected and trusted. Being real is freeing. When you love and respect yourself for who you are, you don't need others' approval as much. You become more confident, more respected, and, interestingly, more liked.

So, do you love yourself enough to be authentic? Accept your true self. It's not just freeing; it's deeply fulfilling.

## Being aware OR beware!

Have you ever danced on a speeding bus? That's what dealing with a difficult boss felt like for me, without losing my cool. Here's a tale from the trenches about how understanding my role and its boundaries helped me navigate through this fiery landscape.

Imagine a very difficult boss who can make your career, not a cushion but a cactus. Every meeting is a war field, and feedback sessions like "One Way Street"

So, how did I manage to survive without turning into a human firework? Here's how I did it:

First, I became a Zen master of active listening. But here's the surprising part: by really listening and engaging, I managed to turn those one-sided speeches into productive dialogues.

Second, I perfected the art of the feedback sandwich: compliment, criticize, and compliment. It's like hiding medicine in a dog's treat. My boss never saw it coming, and it worked wonders. This approach allowed me to deliver constructive feedback without triggering defensive reactions.

Third, I documented everything. Emails became my sharp weapon. Every request from my boss and every piece of feedback was carefully documented. This wasn't just for keeping records; it was my shield and sword in the battles we often faced.

I did not forget to practice empathy. I tried to see things from his perspective, which wasn't easy. The shoes were tight and uncomfortable, honestly causing blisters on my persistence. Yet, this helped me understand the pressures my boss was under. It didn't excuse their behavior, but it helped me respond thoughtfully instead of reacting imprudently.

Understanding the boundaries of my role and respecting those of others played a crucial part in these strategies. Knowing where my responsibilities began and ended, and recognizing the limits of my boss's temperament and authority, allowed me to navigate through my daily tasks more effectively. This helped in maintaining my sanity and in advancing my career by demonstrating resilience, strategic communication, and a clear understanding of workplace dynamics.

By mastering these aspects, I was able to survive my "dance moves on a speeding bus" and thrive, gaining skills that propelled my career forward in unexpected ways.

### *Turning Challenges into Opportunities*

So, what's the takeaway from navigating through tough challenges with a difficult boss? It's that you can't control others, but you can control how you respond. This lesson is invaluable. A difficult boss, while challenging, can sometimes teach you more about patience, strategy, and empathy than any easy-going leader ever could.

Dealing with such challenges not only tests your limits but also expands them. You learn that the true measure of your professional growth often comes from how well you manage adversity. Each interaction with a difficult boss was a lesson in self-control and a chance to refine my approach to communication and problem-solving.

These experiences have taught me that in the face of difficulty, our greatest tool is our ability to choose our response. By choosing to respond with understanding and strategy, I turned potential conflicts into opportunities for personal and professional development.

*Remember, every challenging moment at work is an opportunity to learn and enhance your capabilities, making you more equipped for any future challenges.*

## Your job seems like a pain

Sometimes, you might find yourself in a job that doesn't feel right. Recognizing this is important, and taking action to address it is even more crucial.

It's common to feel out of place in a job. Maybe the tasks don't match your skills or passions, or the work environment isn't right for you. Admitting these feelings is the first step toward finding a better fit.

I once had a job where I felt stuck. The work was clear, but it didn't excite me. Each day felt repetitive, and I felt its monotonous. I realized staying in this role would hurt my growth and happiness.

To address this, I talked with my manager about my career goals and how they matched my current job. Being honest with myself and my boss was key. Discussed my concerns and looked for other opportunities within the company. This talk opened doors to new projects that suited me better.

## Demonstrate your strengths

After realizing your role isn't the best fit, it's important to take initiative. Show that you're willing to go beyond your duties to find or create opportunities that match your strengths and passions.

For example, I saw a problem with our team's project management. Even though it wasn't part of my job, I worked on improving it. I developed new tools and strategies to make our work smoother. My efforts were noticed. This not only helped our team but also showed my problem-solving skills and initiative to the higher-ups.

Taking on new projects or suggesting improvements shows you are proactive and capable. It shows your value to the organization and opens new career paths. Colleagues who started in traditional roles but took on new projects outside their job descriptions enriched their careers and brought fresh ideas to our organization. They created opportunities by being proactive and showing what they could do.

Networking with others in your industry can also open new doors. Building relationships with colleagues, mentors, and other professionals can lead to projects or roles that fit your career goals. In my experience, attending industry events and connecting with professionals on LinkedIn helped me find new opportunities and gain valuable insights.

## Staying Motivated and Self-Aware

Remember, it's not your job to convince others to support your growth. Your main job is to stay true to your path and yourself. Use what you are learning to become the best version of yourself. Focus on being happy, grateful, successful, and kind. Often, your success will inspire others eventually.

In a world with many people, if you keep exploring and stay open, you're likely to find those who will support, inspire, and challenge you to do better. These connections are invaluable as they support your growth and encourage you to push the boundaries of your current role.

So keep yourself motivated and don't hesitate to celebrate your achievements. Recognizing your own successes can fuel your journey and keep you driven, regardless of external validation. By staying proactive and showing what you can do, you can go beyond your defined role and create new opportunities for growth and success.

## Don't take it all seriously- Allow humor to flow in

The other day, someone said to me, *"Kavitha, I love your sense of humor. How can you pull it off being in a leadership role?"* It made me smile and think about why humor, especially in how we present ourselves, is so crucial for success in today's corporate environment.

Honestly, having a sense of humor as a leader is essential. It keeps things from becoming too draining. Imagine trying to navigate through a tough project or a stressful meeting—humor can be a lifesaver. It's like having a secret weapon that can defuse tension and help everyone feel more at ease. Suddenly, a stiff meeting room can lighten up, and people start engaging more openly.

I've found that being able to laugh at myself helps not just me but my whole team. It relaxes the atmosphere and clears our minds for better problem-solving. Insisting on being perfect all the time is exhausting because let's face it, no one is perfect—not even the most polished leader.

Plus, when you have a bit of humor in a presentation or a meeting, it's incredible how it shifts the energy. People sit up, they listen, they connect. It's about making everyone comfortable enough to share ideas and challenges openly.

But here's the catch—you've got to know the boundaries. Humor is fantastic, but knowing when to be serious is just as important. It's about striking that balance where you don't overdo it and lose the respect of your team.

This will let you adapt, react positively to feedback, and meet your team where they are. It turns out that being able to chuckle at yourself might just make you a more effective leader.

*What do you think?*

*Does humor play a part in your view of effective leadership?*

*"It's not what we think or say but what we do that truly defines us."*

– Jane Austen

CHAPTER 4

# YOU BECOME WHAT YOU DO—NOT WHAT YOU THINK!

Women are so powerful that we can become anything when we decide.

90% of the time we women fail to identify a leadership mindset that is within us by default.

Women in the form of Mother, in the form of Sister, in the form of wife, in the form of daughter we are all born leaders, We are born to Lead.

But contradicting in the corporate world, it's hardly 10% who make it to leadership roles due to whatever reasons it may be.

All it takes is enabling your leadership mindset! That's all that is needed.

Have you ever noticed how your small, everyday actions shape who you become? It's not just about what you think or plan to do, but what you actually do every single day. Let me share a story about how I learned this lesson early in my career.

When I first started working, I had no big dreams and no goals. I did not spend time thinking about success and how it would feel. I took actions that gave me confidence to move ahead in my career. Some great leaders noticed the potential and gave me a place at the table and that shaped my career and growing into the leadership role.

I remember feeling overwhelmed with the amount of work but I thoroughly enjoyed being productive. I focused on what I could do every day that could add value to the team and the organization. This shift from thinking to doing made all the difference.

Every choice we make, every task we complete, and every habit we form are the building blocks of who we become. It's not enough to just think about who you want to be; you must live out those aspirations through your actions. Whether it's in our careers, personal lives, or relationships, reaching our full potential is about the daily steps we take.

This isn't just about working hard; it's about working smart and with purpose. It's about making choices that align with our deepest values and pushing ourselves to grow even when it's uncomfortable. Each small step, each consistent action, contributes to the bigger picture of our lives.

## The Power of Consistent Action

Consistent actions are like small seeds that grow into strong habits, defining our character over time. It's not what we think or say we will do that matters, but what we actually do each day. Consistency in our actions builds habits that shape who we are and what we achieve.

When you take consistent actions, you form habits that become second nature. For example, speaking kindly every day becomes a habit that defines you as a supportive and positive person. Telling the truth, even when it's hard, becomes a habit that builds your integrity and credibility. These daily actions might seem small, but over time, they shape your character and how others perceive you.

I remember starting my day with a simple habit: greeting everyone with a smile and a kind word. It might seem unimportant, but this consistent action helped create a positive atmosphere in the office. Colleagues started to mirror this behavior, and soon, our workplace felt more welcoming and supportive. This small, consistent action built a habit that defined my character and positively influenced my work environment.

*Consistent actions lead to long-term success.*

## Aligning Actions with Values

Aligning actions with core values is crucial. It means that what you do every day reflects who you truly are and what you believe in. This alignment builds integrity, empathy, and gratitude, which are key to building a fulfilling life and career.

When actions reflect core values, you live authentically and consistently. This creates trust and respect from those around you and ensures you feel true to yourself. Living out your values in daily actions is about making choices that lead to a meaningful and impactful life.

### *Gratitude*

Gratitude means being thankful and showing appreciation. Recognizing and expressing gratitude can boost morale and foster a positive environment. Simple actions like thanking someone for their help or acknowledging their hard work can go a long way. This makes others feel valued and creates a culture of appreciation and respect. Consistently showing gratitude builds an atmosphere where everyone feels recognized and motivated.

Making it a point to thank the team for their efforts regularly, whether it's a small task or a major project, helps everyone feel appreciated and encouraged.

### *Integrity*

Being honest and having strong moral principles is key. When telling the truth, even when it's hard, credibility is built. People trust those who stand by their word. Integrity is about making sure actions match words. For example, if honesty is valued, actions like admitting mistakes or giving honest feedback should reflect that value. This builds a reputation for reliability and truthfulness.

A time came when admitting a mistake at work was necessary. It wasn't easy, but owning up to it showed colleagues that honesty was valued. They respected more for it, strengthening working relationships.

### *Empathy*

Empathy involves understanding and sharing the feelings of others. By empathizing with others' pain, strong, meaningful connections are created. When genuine care is shown through actions, trust and loyalty are built. For instance, if a colleague is going through a tough time, offering support and understanding can make a significant difference. Actions like these show that compassion is valued and build a supportive community.

## Barriers to Action

In the corporate world, it can be hard to take that first step in being a woman. Sometimes we're afraid of change, or we get too comfortable where we are, even if it's not the best place for us. Other times, we might be tempted by a paycheck and ignore the other, less tangible parts of job satisfaction. Taking action is often easier said than done. Various obstacles can prevent us from moving forward, such as fear, comfort, and doubt. Understanding these barriers and finding ways to overcome them can help us take proactive steps toward our goals.

Fear is one of the biggest barriers to action. It can take many forms: fear of failure, fear of making the wrong decision, or fear of the unknown. This fear can paralyze us, making it difficult to take the first step. For example, you might hesitate to apply for a new job because you're afraid you won't be good enough or won't fit in. This fear keeps you stuck in your current situation, even if it's not fulfilling.

Comfort can also be a significant obstacle. When we're comfortable, we often don't want to disrupt our routine, even if it means missing out on better opportunities. It's easy to stay in a job that doesn't excite you or a routine that doesn't challenge you because it feels safe. But comfort can be a trap that keeps you from growing and achieving your potential.

Doubt can stop us from taking action. When you doubt your abilities or the outcome of your actions, you're less likely to take risks. This doubt can be internal, like questioning your skills, or external, like worrying about what others will think. Doubt creates a mental barrier that's hard to overcome, leaving you stuck in inaction.

## Thinking Big in Action

Thinking big isn't just about having grand ideas; it's about putting those ideas into real actions that move you forward. Here's how you can make that happen in everyday life:

- **Know Your Why:** It's crucial to understand why you're doing what you're doing. This understanding is your foundation. Once you grasp your 'why,' the 'what' and 'how' of your actions become clearer.
- **Take That First Step:** Starting can seem daunting, but often the first step isn't as scary as it seems. Once you begin, momentum builds, and things get easier.
- **Be Consistent, Be Deliberate:** Make progress by being consistent. Each action you take should purposefully align with your bigger goals.
- **Embrace Discomfort, Practice Experimentation:** Get comfortable with being uncomfortable. Try new things, learn from what fails, and understand that each mistake teaches you something valuable.
- **Intelligence is Not Everything, Attitude Counts:** While intelligence is valuable, your attitude often determines your success. A positive and proactive attitude inspires you to learn and overcome challenges.
- **Others Can Pull You Down, Don't Let Them:** Sometimes, people might try to discourage you. Remember, their doubts don't define what you

can achieve. Keep moving forward despite the setbacks.

- **Network is Power, Utilize It:** Strong relationships can open doors. Networking is about more than just meeting people; it's about building meaningful connections that can support you on your journey.
- **Adapt, Then Correct:** Stay flexible and ready to change your approach when needed. If something isn't working, be ready to adjust your methods. Adapting to situations and correcting your course is a key part of making big ideas a reality.

## Staying Calm and Taking Action

Imagine you're on a flight, sitting comfortably as the flight attendant explains safety procedures. She talks about the oxygen mask, instructing everyone to put it on and "breathe normally" if there's an emergency. That always seemed like strange advice to me. How could anyone remain calm enough to breathe normally in such a stressful situation?

Yet, this is actually great advice, not just for emergencies on a plane, but for dealing with big decisions in our careers. When faced with important choices, it's easy to feel overwhelmed, just like you might feel during an airplane emergency.

When this happens, the best thing to do is to take a deep breath and try to relax. This helps clear your mind. With a clearer mind, you can start to think about your decision step by step. What are the benefits and risks?

What might happen next? Breaking it down like this makes the decision less scary and more manageable.

When you're in a high-pressure situation, the first thing to do is take a deep breath. This simple act helps calm your nerves and clears your mind. Imagine being on that airplane, feeling the rush of anxiety as the oxygen masks drop. The instinct might be to panic, but taking a moment to breathe can make all the difference. In your career, this translates to not rushing into decisions without thinking them through. Instead, take a moment to collect your thoughts and calm your emotions.

Once you're calm, start breaking down the decision into smaller, more manageable parts. Think about the benefits and risks of each option. What are the potential outcomes? By examining each step carefully, you can see the bigger picture more clearly. This approach makes the decision-making process less intimidating. It's like dealing with an emergency on a plane: you follow the steps you've been taught, which helps you manage the situation more effectively.

It's important to move at your own pace and not rush. Rushing can lead to mistakes. But if you wait too long, you might miss your chance. Find a middle ground where you can think things through and take action when you need to. Just like on a plane, where rushing to put on your oxygen mask might cause you to fumble, taking your time to do it correctly ensures your safety. In your career, balance is key. Take the time to make informed decisions, but don't delay so long that you miss opportunities.

It's okay to feel unsure sometimes. Everyone does when make big decisions. What's important is that you don't let this fear stop you from moving forward. Uncertainty is a natural part of life. Acknowledge it, but don't let it paralyze you. On a flight, you wouldn't ignore the oxygen mask just because you're unsure of the situation; you would put it on to protect yourself. Similarly, in your career, face your decisions head-on and handle them as best as you can.

When you face big decisions in your career, remember the advice of the flight attendant: breathe normally. Stay calm, assess the situation, and take action. By breaking down your decisions into manageable steps, you can handle them more effectively. Recognize the importance of timing—don't rush, but don't delay unnecessarily. And remember, feeling unsure is normal. What matters is that you move forward despite the uncertainty.

## Taking Initiative

One of the most important lessons in my career has been the value of taking initiative. It's not just about doing your assigned tasks but also about stepping up to do what needs to be done before anyone even asks. Let me share some straightforward truths I've learned and a specific instance where taking initiative made a real difference in my career.

*Valuable Lessons Learned*

Over the years, I've realized several key things that have guided me:

**You need more focus, not more time.** It's essential to zero in on what truly matters instead of wishing there were more hours in the day.

**You need more sleep, not more coffee.** Real rest beats caffeine any day because it refreshes your mind and body, making you more effective in everything you do.

**You need more action, not more information.** In today's world, it's easy to feel like you need to know everything before you start anything. But often, the best way to learn is by doing.

**You need more ownership, not more support.** It's great to have help, but ultimately, taking full responsibility for your projects is what leads to meaningful progress.

**You need more consistency, not more help.** Regular effort on your part sets the foundation for success better than sporadic assistance from others.

**You need more self-assurance, not more applause.** Believing in yourself is crucial because confidence from within keeps you going even when external praise is scarce.

*Traits of a 'High Performer'- Make sure that's YOU!*

**When you hear someone described as a "high performer,"** it might surprise you to learn that they often display qualities that are subtle yet incredibly effective in the workplace:

**She's quieter in meetings than most.** This allows her to listen carefully, understand deeply, and speak only when she has something valuable to add.

**She focuses on outcomes, not time worked.** Her goal is effectiveness, not merely being seen; she measures success by results achieved.

**She focuses on learning over blaming others.** When mistakes happen, she looks for solutions and lessons, rather than wasting time on pointing fingers.

**She helps other colleagues without them asking for help.** She's proactive in her support, making her a valued member of any team.

**She's a leader but doesn't necessarily have the job title.** Her influence and guidance are natural, stemming from her competence and fairness, not from a formal authority.

**She does work she enjoys overdoing it for money.** Passion drives her choices, leading to higher satisfaction and better performance.

**She shares stories and experiences on LinkedIn.** She understands the power of networking and personal branding in building a career.

**She has an optimistic attitude.** Her positivity makes her resilient and a pleasure to work alongside.

**She's open-minded with a growth mindset.** Always ready to learn and adapt, she sees every challenge as an opportunity to grow.

High performers are not the loudest or most visible in a room. Instead, they excel in the small things with consistency and excellence. They are not loud or arrogant; their actions, attitudes, and results speak for themselves, establishing their high-performance status.

## Learning from the Past for Future Success

Reflecting on past actions is crucial for personal and professional growth. It's not just about acknowledging what you've done; it's about understanding the impact of those actions and using that knowledge to make better decisions in the future. This process of reflection has been a vital part of my journey, especially during a significant transition in my life 13 years ago.

Back then, I made a bold choice to quit my job without having another offer lined up. It was a decision driven by the need to prioritize my family, though I was also preparing for my PMP certification. This period was challenging but transformative, and it taught me a lot about the value of reflection.

During this time, a friend played a crucial role in my professional life. He wasn't just a friend but a well-wisher who believed in me when.

He consistently kept in touch, encouraging me to stay connected with the professional world even when I was focused on my family.

He pushed me to update my resume and motivated me to start applying for jobs again. His encouragement was a reminder of the importance of taking proactive steps, even when you're unsure of the outcome.

He made sure I was aware of industry changes, which helped me stay relevant even after a break. His updates ensured I didn't fall behind and felt prepared to re-enter the job market.

When an opportunity arose that matched my skills and career level, he didn't hesitate to refer me. His support didn't just stop with encouragement; he actively contributed to my comeback.

Thanks to his efforts and belief in me, I landed a job that allowed me to return to the workforce with dignity and pride. This experience wasn't just about getting a job—it was about regaining my professional confidence.

From this experience, I learned the importance of having supportive people in your life and the impact of paying that support forward. Reflecting on this phase showed me the value of loyalty, encouragement, and active help. It taught me to be the kind of friend to others that he was to me—someone who not only stands by you in tough times but also plays an active role in helping you succeed.

## The Value of Reflection

Reflection isn't just about looking back; it's about learning and growing. It helps you understand what worked and what didn't, and why. By reflecting on past experiences, you can gain insights that guide your future actions.

When you reflect on your past actions, ask yourself these questions:

- *What did I learn from this experience?*
- *How did my actions affect the outcome?*
- *What could I have done differently?*
- *How can I apply these lessons to future situations?*

Learning from the past gives you the confidence to move forward. It shows that you can handle challenges and come out stronger on the other side. When faced with new decisions or obstacles, remember the lessons you've learned and trust in your ability to navigate through them.

Reflection, support, and continuous learning are key to success. By looking back and learning from your experiences, you can make better decisions and achieve your goals. This process helps you grow and strengthens your resilience and adaptability.

## A Little Persistence Goes a Long Way

I remember coming back from a personal trip, flying from Bangkok to Bengaluru. It had been a long day. The flight was delayed by four hours, so to pass the time, I grabbed a meal at Burger King at Suvarnabhumi Airport. Once we finally boarded and the plane took off, I settled into my seat and started feeling chilly. That's when I realized I was missing my jacket—the one I had worn all day at the airport.

In a rush to the board, I had left it at the restaurant while taking photos. Realizing this, I felt really irritated with myself. It was my favorite jacket, a gift from my husband. I thought it was gone for good.

Came back home, still upset with myself for being so forgetful, and an idea hit me. Why not call the restaurant? It seemed a bit silly at first—calling a busy fast-food place in a huge airport about a lost jacket. But I decided to try anyway. I got a colleague from Bangkok to help me communicate, and we called Burger King. At first, they said they hadn't found anything. I wasn't ready to give up, something made me keep going.

I sent an email to the branch manager with pictures of the jacket I had taken at the restaurant. I also explained how much it meant to me. I didn't expect much, but I had to try. The next day, to my surprise, the manager replied. They had found my jacket after all! They even sent pictures to make sure it was the right one and then asked for my address to send it back.

I couldn't believe it. It felt like no less than a miracle. I was so grateful that they took the time to look for it and send it back to me.

How a little effort and persistence can pay off in ways you never expected. Sometimes, just taking that extra step, even when it seems unlikely to work, can lead to surprising and wonderful outcomes.

*You Become What You Do—Not What You Think!*

Remember, *it's the daily actions, no matter how small, that define us. You become what you do, not what you think. Make your actions count, and let them lead you to the person you aspire to be.*

*"Women don't need to be empowered;*
*they just need equal opportunities"*

– Kavitha Ramakrishnappa

CHAPTER 5

# MEN AT WORK!

## *Strong Men Support Women; Weak Men Target women*

I have had strong support from men in my career in all the good and organic ways. I owe it to those strong men for supporting me in my career and believing in me when they acted as catalysts for the opportunities that came my way.

My Dad, my Brother, my Husband, my Son have been great pillars of support for me Personally & Professionally. My Managers too who gave me equal opportunity and not just shoo off me because of my gender.

As the saying goes, where there is good, there will be bad too. My career has never been smooth; it's always been a roller coaster. I feel greatly humbled and full of gratitude for the way it started and the way it's going.

Great leaders don't care about your gender—they just see your potential and give you opportunities. However, others reject you outright just because you're a woman. In some organizations, this kind of bias is ignored. They may claim to support gender diversity, saying they reserve 30% of leadership roles for women, but in reality, they reject women profiles outright without even giving an opportunity for an interview. I have seen this and have challenged and haven't got any support or convincing answers.

Sometimes onsite opportunities are not given to women, just because of her gender. Forget about the onsite opportunities, Leadership titles are not given to women as much as they are given to men with same experience and skills. Who should we raise such concerns with? Even if raised, it just falls into deaf ears and blind eyes.

It's crucial to recognize the support from those who see beyond gender and value true potential. At the same time, we must also acknowledge and address the challenges posed by those who still hold onto old biases. The journey towards gender equality in the workplace is ongoing, shaped by both the allies who lift us and the obstacles we overcome along the way.

## Experiencing different worlds

- I worked in a company that had no women in leadership roles at all. I also worked in a company that had women leaders across each department and each vertical.
- I worked in a company that laid off a person because she was a woman. I also worked in a company that hired me not because of my gender but because of what I could bring to the table.
- I worked in a company where women were excluded from making big decisions. I also worked in a company where women were included in all decisions.
- I worked in a company where the VP used F words during meetings even when women were around. I also worked in a company where the

VP/CTO respected everyone's ideas and made sure they were implemented.

- I worked in a company where women were not part of team lunches or dinners. I also worked in a company where women were included in all outings and celebrations.
- I worked in a company where one-on-one meetings were canceled and career interests were never discussed because she was a woman. I also worked in a company where C-level executives scheduled meetings to discuss my career and interests.

It's all about those strong men and women who make things happen by setting aside gender bias. They see potential and talent, not gender. They support and uplift, creating an environment where everyone can thrive- Are you one among those strong men? If you are, be proud of yourself. World needs more people like you.

While it's important to focus on the positive aspects of our experiences, it's equally important to reflect on where you are and if it's the right place for you. If you find yourself in an environment where you are not valued or respected, it might be time to consider if it's the right fit for you.

Most of the men support their mother, sister, wife daughter but what happens when it comes to a female colleague? They don't support in any means be it equal pay, equal opportunities, equal level, or equal roles- why these double standards?? Remember what goes around comes around- isn't it?

## Sign Board & Men

Have you ever noticed a signboard that says, *"MEN AT WORK"?* It's funny how men need a sign to say they are working. Women don't put up a sign board; we just do our job without announcing it. But that's a real problem, you see.

*For women, it takes a lot.*

- *You will have to be visible.*
- *You will have to add real value.*
- *You will have to be accountable.*
- *You will have to own your work to make it work.*
- *You will have to design your career without waiting for others to do it for you.*

In your career, it's important to let others know about your achievements and what you are working on. Go beyond your role by adding the required value.

Taking responsibility for your actions and decisions is key. Be reliable and follow through on your commitments. When you take ownership of your work, you take pride in what you do and stand by your results. Set clear goals and make a plan to achieve them. Identify the skills and experiences you need and look for ways to develop them. Take charge of your career by being strategic and intentional about your growth and development.

*So, how do you do it?*

Believe your instincts! That's the key.

Trusting yourself is the first step to success. It's about having confidence in your judgment and knowing that you can handle whatever comes your way.

Sit down with yourself for at least 30 minutes a day and reflect on what you want. Ask yourself questions like: What are my goals? What steps do I need to take? What have I accomplished today? This daily reflection helps you stay focused and aligned with your aspirations.

Think about what you need to do to get what you want. Break down your goals into manageable steps and take action. Reflecting daily helps you understand what's working and what's not, allowing you to adjust your approach as needed.

Identify who can help you and who cannot. Surround yourself with people who believe in you and your dreams. Seek out mentors, colleagues, and friends who can offer guidance, support, and honest feedback. Be cautious of those who might discourage you or undermine your confidence. One major factor to consider is whether your thought processes match. The right support comes from those who understand and share your vision and values.

Be mindful of who you share your dreams with—not everyone will support you. Know your people! Share your aspirations with those who genuinely care about your success and well-being. They are the ones who will stand by you, offering encouragement and constructive criticism.

Remember, having a strong support system can make all the difference in achieving your goals.

## 'Softer' Roles are for Women

Women are frequently side-lined into 'softer' roles. Today, such practices are illegal in many countries, reflecting a more inclusive and diverse approach to recruitment.

Have you noticed that the HR head role is usually a woman in many organizations? Have you ever thought about why that is or asked any leaders in the organization?

I dared to ask this question to my manager, who was a Senior Vice President. He wasn't prepared, but when asked, he didn't hesitate to answer. He said, "Oh, HR in the organization is powerless because the functional heads make all decisions. Any decisions HR has to make need approval from all the other heads in the organization, except for smaller decisions that have no significant impact." It's the powerless roles most of the time.

I know some HR professionals might not agree with this statement, but there are exceptions, and one cannot deny the hard truth.

Women often end up in roles like HR, which are perceived as supportive rather than strategic. While HR is essential for any organization, it's often seen as less influential compared to other departments. This perception can limit the opportunities for women to advance into more strategic and decision-making roles.

Addressing this issue requires a change in mindset and organizational culture. It's important to recognize the value that women bring to all roles, not just the ones traditionally considered as 'soft.' By breaking these stereotypes, decision-makers should create a more balanced workplace where everyone has the chance to lead and make significant contributions.

## Open Communication Creates Magic

In the past, information in organizations only flowed from the top down. Employees at lower levels rarely had the chance to give input or feedback. This way of managing killed new ideas and made many feel undervalued and unheard.

Today, workplaces are different. Now, talking and working together is encouraged at all levels. This change values everyone's thoughts and ideas, recognizing that everyone has something important to contribute.

As a leader, it's crucial to encourage open communication. This means making sure everyone, no matter their position, can share their thoughts and ideas. When people feel heard, they trust the organization more and are more likely to give their best efforts.

Leaders who promote open communication build a positive culture. This culture values everyone and ensures all feel included. It not only improves the work environment but also drives success and innovation. It breaks down barriers, builds trust, and makes sure everyone's voice is heard. By promoting open talk, leaders can make their workplaces better for everyone.

This approach also helps tackle gender discrimination. When everyone can speak up, it's easier to spot and address biases. This creates a respectful workplace for all employees.

## Gender! It's All About the Mindset

Gender is more than just being male or female; it's about how we perceive and treat each other. In the workplace, our mindset about gender can shape everything. It influences who gets hired, who gets promoted, and who feels valued. This can show up in many ways, including:

**Pay Gap:** Women often earn less than men for doing the same work or having similar roles. Despite having the same qualifications and experience, women frequently receive lower salaries. This gap can affect not just their immediate earnings but also their long-term financial stability, including retirement savings.

**Promotion and Career Development:** Women may be overlooked for promotions or miss out on opportunities to advance in their careers. Often, women find themselves stuck in mid-level positions while men climb the ladder. This can be due to biases that question women's commitment to their careers or assumptions about their ability to lead.

**Harassment:** This includes sexual harassment or creating a hostile work environment because of gender. Women might face unwanted advances, inappropriate comments, or even threats. Such behavior not only affects their mental and emotional well-being but also their job performance and career progression.

**Stereotyping:** Making assumptions about what roles and tasks women and men are suited for, based on gender rather than individual skills. For example, assuming women are better suited for administrative roles and men for technical roles. These stereotypes limit opportunities and discourage women from pursuing careers in certain fields.

**Workplace Policies and Practices:** Sometimes, policies unintentionally favor one gender over another. For example, parental leave policies that primarily support mothers but not fathers, or lack of flexible work options that can help both men and women balance work and family responsibilities. These policies can make it difficult for women to manage their careers and personal lives.

Addressing Gender discrimination requires efforts from both organizations and individuals. It means creating and enforcing policies that promote equality, providing training on unconscious bias and harassment, building a welcoming workplace culture, and making sure everyone has equal opportunities. *So, how do we do this?*

*To get more women into leadership roles, we need a clear and strategic approach. Here are some steps that can help:*

First, take a good look at the current situation. Examine your organization's leadership demographics. See if there are any gaps or imbalances in the number of women in leadership roles compared to their overall presence in the workforce.

Next, make sure top leadership is on board. Senior leaders must be committed to gender diversity and inclusion. This commitment should be visible in their statements, policies, and ACTIONS that support promoting women into leadership roles.

Then, review and update policies. Look at your current policies and practices to find any barriers that might prevent women from advancing in their careers. This includes recruitment, promotion, pay, flexible work options, parental leave, and mentoring programs.

Set clear gender diversity goals. Establish specific, measurable targets for increasing the number of women in leadership positions. Include these goals in your organization's strategic plans and regularly check progress to ensure you are on track.

Provide growth opportunities across the organization. Don't just have empowerment programs for the sake of it. Women are already empowered, all they need is equal opportunities and make them inclusive.

Encourage inclusive leadership. Train current leaders to value diverse perspectives and contributions. Teach them about unconscious bias and how to communicate inclusively. Create a supportive environment for all employees.

Build a supportive culture. Make your workplace a place where work-life balance, flexibility, and inclusivity are valued.

Ensure fair pay. Regularly review salaries within your organization to make sure women are paid fairly compared to men in similar roles.

Celebrate achievements and role models. Recognize and celebrate the successes of women leaders in your organization. Share their stories to inspire others and show the value of gender diversity in leadership.

Keep track of progress. Continuously monitor how well you are doing in reaching your gender diversity goals. Regularly assess the effectiveness of your initiatives. Use feedback from women employees to improve your strategies and address any new challenges.

## Note to My Younger Self

*"When you pick up a job next time, make sure that the organization has more than just a handful of women in leadership roles. I wish someone had told me this earlier ☺."*

When you're starting, it's easy to overlook the importance of having women in leadership positions. You might focus on the job itself, the salary, or the company's reputation. But having women in leadership roles is crucial. It shows that the company values diversity and inclusion, and it means you'll have role models who understand your experiences and challenges.

In my career, I've learned that working in an environment where women hold leadership roles makes a huge difference. It's inspiring and empowering to see women leading and making impactful decisions. It creates a culture where everyone's voice is heard and respected.

So, next time you're considering a job, take a look at the leadership team. Are there women in those positions? If not, think twice. Aim to work in places that truly value and promote gender diversity. This will not only support your growth but also help create a more inclusive and fairer workplace for everyone.

*Remember, where you work can greatly affect your career and your happiness. Choose wisely and find a place that values and supports women.*

***Men at Leadership roles- Are you listening???***

*When you mute women at work place,*
*you will never get to know full story.*
*It remains half-baked information forever*

– Kavitha Ramakrishnappa

CHAPTER 6

# MUTING HER VOICE

During a meeting with Senior VPs and Directors (all male), discussing a solution for a client requirement, the discussion extended well past forty-five minutes with no clear resolution in sight. Despite waiting for an opportunity to contribute, I found no opening to voice my perspective. Eventually, I gently interrupted, stating, "I'd like to share my viewpoint." Everyone paused to hear me out.

However, less than five minutes into my contribution, someone muted me without my knowledge. It took me over ten seconds to realize that a Senior VP had intentionally muted me while I was still speaking.

I unmuted myself and pointed out, "Someone muted me while I was speaking." To my surprise, the group laughed off the incident and resumed their discussion.

In the end, my proposed solution was adopted, though it was credited under their names.

This incident stayed with me for long time and made me stop attending meetings where I'm muted and not being heard. This is not just my story, there are millions of women who are going through this trauma every day and sadly this culture is "normalized" in most of the boardrooms.

Experiencing such a situation in a professional setting is not only disheartening but also indicative of broader issues concerning respect, inclusion, and the recognition of contributions based on merit. Here's how this scenario can be reflected upon and addressed:

The incident described highlights several concerning aspects:

1. **Disregard for Contributions**: Despite waiting patiently for an opportunity to contribute and speaking up when it seemed appropriate, your input was not only disregarded but actively suppressed by muting you. This action dismisses your expertise and perspective, undermining your role in the discussion.

2. **Lack of Respect**: Muting someone while they are speaking is not only disrespectful but also undermines the norms of professional courtesy and equitable participation in meetings. It demonstrates a power dynamic where certain voices are prioritized over others based on gender.

3. **Cultural and Organizational Norms**: The fact that the group laughed off my assertion of being muted suggests a dismissive attitude towards my experience and concerns. This could indicate entrenched cultural norms within the organization where such behaviours are tolerated or even normalized.

4. **Recognition and Credit**: It is particularly concerning that despite your proposed solution being finalized, credit was not attributed to you. This reflects a broader issue of lack of recognition for contributions made by women voices in decision-making processes.

## How to handle such incidents?

- **Document the Incident**: Keep a record of what transpired, including details of who was present, what was discussed, and how my input was treated. This documentation may be helpful if you decide to address the issue formally within your organization.
- **Seek Support**: Consider discussing the incident with a trusted colleague, mentor, or HR representative who may provide guidance on how to address such situations effectively within your organization's structure.
- **Advocate for Change**: If comfortable and appropriate, raise the issue with your manager, HR, or another appropriate authority within the organization. Articulate your concerns about respectful communication and equitable participation in meetings, emphasizing the importance of recognizing diverse perspectives.
- **Build Allies**: Engage with allies within your organization who share your commitment to diversity, equity, and inclusion. Collective voices often have more impact in driving cultural change and promoting a more inclusive work environment.
- **Personal Development**: Focus on continuing to develop your skills and expertise. Your contributions are valuable and should not be overshadowed. Seek opportunities to showcase your capabilities and ensure your voice is heard and acknowledged.

Addressing incidents of this nature requires both individual courage and collective effort to challenge existing norms and promote a workplace culture that values and respects every employee's contribution.

My brother guided me rightly: ALWAYS keep Emotions aside while dealing such situations.

## Shhhhhh! Silence please!!

Imagine trying to keep a woman quiet—good luck with that! Silencing a woman isn't just about turning down the volume on her voice; it's a complex dance of power plays and outdated societal norms. It's like trying to shush a tornado: futile and kind of ridiculous.

When we talk about silencing women, we're not just talking about literally stopping her from speaking. Oh no, it goes much deeper. It's like playing a never-ending game of "Quiet, Please!" in the realms of social interaction, cultural representation, and systemic inequality. Think of it as the world's most annoying concert, where the biases and prejudices are the headliners and her voice is the opening act that no one hears.

Picture this: a woman's brilliant idea gets a shrug in the boardroom, her insightful question is brushed off in the classroom, and her confident assertion is picked apart like a poorly cooked Thanksgiving turkey in public forums. The media? Well, they either ignore her story or blow it up like it's the next big scandal, all while keeping stereotypes snugly in place.

In personal relationships, it's even worse. Her assertiveness is labeled as aggression (yikes!), her passion is seen as irrationality (double yikes!), and her vulnerability? That's mistaken for weakness. This isn't just annoying; it's career-limiting, opportunity-shrinking, and narrative-skewing madness.

Yet, despite these absurd challenges, her voice is like a stubborn cat—it persists. You can try to hush her, but she'll just find another way to be heard. She'll whisper in solidarity or roar in defiance. She'll climb over those barriers like a ninja and resonate in the hearts and minds of anyone who's had enough of the silence.

Her voice is in the gender equality movements, the advocacy for women's rights, and every courageous act that gives a giant middle finger to the forces trying to keep her quiet.

To tackle this silencing isn't just about being polite; it's about demanding equity and justice. It's about saying goodbye to ingrained biases and making sure her voice gets the mic it deserves. We need to create spaces where her voice isn't just heard but celebrated, where her contributions aren't just acknowledged but applauded.

In other words, it's time to crank up the volume and let her rock the stage.

## Women at Boardrooms

While significant progress has been made in increasing the representation and treatment of women in corporate boardrooms, challenges remain. Addressing unconscious biases, breaking down networking barriers, and promoting work-life balance are crucial steps towards achieving gender parity. Continued efforts from policymakers, corporations, and advocacy groups are essential to create an environment where women can thrive in leadership roles and contribute to corporate success. The journey towards gender equality in boardrooms is ongoing, but the positive trends indicate a promising future.

Historically, corporate boardrooms have been male-dominated spaces, reflecting broader societal norms and gender roles that limited women's participation in leadership and decision-making. Over the past few decades, significant strides have been made toward gender equality, but challenges remain.

## Challenges Faced by Women in Boardrooms

1. **Unconscious Bias:** Women often face unconscious biases that question their competence and suitability for leadership roles. These biases can manifest in various ways, including the underestimation of women's contributions and a tendency to favor male candidates for board positions.
2. **Gender Stereotypes:** Traditional gender stereotypes that view men as more decisive and women as more emotional can negatively impact perceptions of female board members. These stereotypes can influence both the selection process and the dynamics within the boardroom.
3. **Double Bind:** Women in leadership often face a "double bind" where they must balance assertiveness with warmth. Being too assertive can lead to negative judgments, while not being assertive enough can result in being overlooked.
4. **Networking Barriers:** Networking is crucial for board appointments, but women often have

less access to influential networks compared to their male counterparts. This can limit their opportunities for being considered for board roles.

5. **Work-Life Balance**: Women frequently juggle professional responsibilities with greater domestic and caregiving roles, making it challenging to meet the demands of high-level board positions.

## Progress and Positive Trends

1. **Legislative and Policy Initiatives**: Several countries have implemented policies and quotas to increase female representation on boards. For instance, Norway mandates that 40% of board members must be women. Similar measures are in place in other European countries and are being considered elsewhere.
2. **Corporate Commitments**: Many companies are actively working to promote gender diversity at the board level. Initiatives include setting targets for female representation, implementing mentorship programs, and ensuring diverse candidate slates for board appointments.
3. **Research and Advocacy**: Organizations like Catalyst and McKinsey & Company produce research highlighting the business case for gender diversity in leadership. Studies show that companies with diverse boards perform better financially and exhibit superior innovation and decision-making.

4. **Role Models and Mentors**: The presence of successful female board members provides role models for aspiring women leaders. Mentorship and sponsorship programs help women navigate their careers and prepare for board roles.
5. **Changing Corporate Culture**: There is a growing recognition of the importance of inclusive leadership and a shift towards more equitable corporate cultures. This cultural shift is gradually changing attitudes towards women in boardrooms

Unfortunately, all of the above is seen only on papers but yet to put into practice

## Do Women really need empowerment?

The irony of men disempowering and then empowering women underscores the complexity of social change.

While men have historically held power and often perpetuated systems of inequality, many also play crucial roles in advancing gender equality.

True empowerment of women requires both acknowledging past and present injustices and working collaboratively to create a more just and equitable society.

It is a continuous process that involves challenging existing power dynamics and ensuring that women have the autonomy and resources to thrive not only on papers but also in practice.

- **Complicity and Change**: The reality is that individuals within any group, including men, can be both complicit in and opposed to oppressive systems. Some men may consciously or unconsciously perpetuate gender inequalities, while others actively work to dismantle them.

- **Power Redistribution**: Genuine empowerment involves redistributing power and resources, which can be uncomfortable and challenging for those who hold privilege. True allies in gender equality recognize the need for systemic change rather than just symbolic gestures.

Yes, women need empowerment. Empowerment is essential for achieving gender equality and ensuring that women have the same opportunities and rights as men.

At the same time, Men need to be trained how to handle empowered women so that women are treated equal, equal opportunities are given, equal pay is ensured, leadership roles are assigned, unbiased promotions are practiced.

For those who are organising "Women empowerment programs" its high time to start training men as well.

*"Your story is what you have,
tell it to the world authentically"*

– Kavitha Ramakrishnappa

CHAPTER 7

# PEEK INTO MY WORLD

Power comes from within. It's about knowing who you are and what you stand for. It's about trusting yourself even when things get tough. I've faced many challenges, but through it all, I've learned that my strength comes from within. It's not about being perfect; it's about being true to yourself and owning your power.

*I might not be perfect, but I am powerful. And I own it.*

Every one of us has a story filled with choices and moments that test us. This part of my book is about those times in my life. It's about the decisions I made and how they led me to where I am today. It's a peek into my world, showing not just the good times but also the challenges and how I handled them.

I've learned something important through all this: you are your own strongest supporter. Whether it was deciding to take a tough job, standing up for what I believe in, or finding my way through unexpected problems, the biggest lessons came from trusting myself.

Here, you'll read about real things that happened to me—how I dealt with them and what I learned. This isn't just about sharing my victories and the hard work and tough days that got me there. I hope by sharing this, you see how believing in yourself can help you overcome anything.

*Her head held high,*

*and looking everyone in the eye,*

*Unafraid of anyone because.*

*of innate integrity,*

*Possession assuredness,*

*born of courage of conviction,*

*The Modern Woman never feels inferior to any!*

These lines by Mahakavi Bharathiyar beautifully capture what it means to be a modern woman—strong, confident, and true to herself. Today's women carry themselves with confidence and integrity, believing in their values and abilities without feeling inferior to anyone.

In today's world, we have empowered women so much but have forgotten to prepare men to handle those empowered women.

It's not just about equal rights; it's about equal participation, recognition, and influence in all spheres of life. Empowerment means having the freedom to make choices, the strength to voice opinions, and the opportunity to pursue dreams with the same fervor as anyone else.

Modern empowerment is about breaking the traditional molds that have long defined and confined women's roles. It's about women leading companies, making groundbreaking scientific discoveries, influencing political landscapes, and inspiring change that reshapes the world. But it's also about the quieter strengths: educating children, managing households, and making daily decisions that keep the fabric of society strong.

However, empowerment is not just a personal journey. It's also about creating supportive communities that uplift other women. It involves challenging the stereotypes and biases that hinder women's progress and replacing them with new norms that value and celebrate women's contributions and potential.

Seasoned women leaders mentoring young women bring powerful perspectives and wisdom, preparing the next generation to climb higher and reach further.

This journey of empowerment is ongoing. Each step forward is a step toward a world where no woman feels inferior, and where every woman's potential is recognized and nurtured. The modern woman is not just a participant in this journey; she is a leader and a way for change.

As we reflect on the courage and conviction of women today, we see a future bright with promise—a future where women lead with their heads held high, not just in victory but in every step of their journey.

### *Where Did It All Start?*

She is the foundation of my strength and the heart of my world.

She is my rock.

She is my inspiration.

She is my Miss World.

She is my cheerleader.

She is my forever friend.

She is the tablet for all my pains

Reflecting on my journey, I sometimes wonder when I transitioned from being 'Dad's princess' to 'Mama's girl.' It's hard to pinpoint the exact moment, but it feels like it was always meant to be this way. My mom has been a constant source of love and support, guiding me through life's challenges with wisdom and patience. She taught me the value of integrity and the strength that comes from knowing and standing by your beliefs.

When I think back to my childhood, my mom was always there, a steady presence in my life. She was the one who helped me with most difficult subjects, silently encouraged me to be strong, and picked me up when I fell. Her strength was quiet but powerful, and it shaped the person I am today.

My mom's lessons went beyond words. She led by example. I remember watching her handle difficult situations with calmness and patience. This taught me that strength doesn't always have to be loud; sometimes, it's in the quiet resolve to keep going no matter what.

One of the most important lessons my mom taught me was the importance of integrity. She always emphasized that doing the right thing is more important than taking the easy way out. This lesson has guided me through many difficult decisions in my life. Whenever I face a tough choice, I think about what my mom would do, and it helps me find the courage to do what's right.

Her belief in me has been a source of incredible strength. Even when I doubted myself, she never did. She always told me that I could achieve anything I set my mind to, and her faith in me made me believe it too. This support has been my anchor, helping me stay grounded and focused on my goals.

Looking back, I realize that my mom's influence is in every part of my life. She is the reason I am confident, resilient, and unafraid to stand up for what I believe in. Her love and support have been the greatest gifts I could ever receive, and they continue to inspire me every day.

## Plan B

Growing up, my dreams were as big and varied as the sky. I imagined myself in many roles—a Surgeon, a War Journalist, a Professor, a Criminal Lawyer, even as ambitious as a CEO or the Prime Minister. These were my Plan A, the dreams I daydreamed about pursuing with passion.

However, my dad, always practical and insightful, guided me towards a more grounded approach. He supported my dreams but also instilled in me the value of a solid education. He got me to agree that I could chase all those dreams, but only after I secured my academic degree and Master's. That became my Plan B.

He made sure this Plan B was not just a fallback but a strong, viable path that could support any future I chose. Thanks to his wisdom, I came to see the importance of having a Plan B. Life, as I've learned, is mostly about navigating Plan Bs. It's about adapting and finding value in the paths we end up on, even if they weren't our first choice.

So always have a Plan B, one that is good enough to live a fulfilling life. This plan should give you a foundation to build upon, no matter which direction your life takes. Plan B isn't a compromise; it's a safeguard, a strategy that ensures you keep moving forward even when unexpected changes happen.

## Leadership to me

Throughout my over 22 years of working in corporate, I've noticed something quite telling—I've never had the chance to report to a female manager or leader. This absence made me think deeply about the kind of leader I wanted to be and the examples I saw around me.

My mother, my guiding star, used to say, "If you can't find the person you are looking for, be one!"

Her words resonated with me not just in my personal life but also in my professional journey. So when I stepped into the corporate world, I took her advice to heart. I didn't choose Leadership- Leadership chose me. I sought them out and embraced them from the early days of my career.

I'm not entirely sure how many lives I've touched or influenced along the way. Yet I strive to lead with honesty and integrity, qualities I hold dear even when I find they are lacking in others around me. It's these values that have shaped my approach to leadership and guided my interactions with my team and peers.

To me, leadership has never been about gender, title, or a specific role. It's about the mindset. It's about how you approach challenges, inspire your team, and drive change. A true leader is someone who creates an environment where others feel valued and empowered to achieve their best.

## Building Strong Teams

Building a strong team is about understanding and balancing the different abilities of each member. It's like finding the right place for each piece in a puzzle. When you see someone's strength as a way to make up for another's weakness, the whole team becomes stronger—without taking advantage of anyone.

To do this effectively, you must recognize what each person does best and how these abilities can help others who might not have the same skills. For example, if one team member is great at coming up with big ideas but not so good at details, pairing them with someone who thrives on organization and precision can lead to better results for everyone.

Here's how you can build a team where everyone's abilities are used well:

- **Open Communication:** Encourage everyone to share their thoughts and feelings about the work they're doing. This openness helps you understand their strengths and weaknesses better.
- **Assign Roles Thoughtfully:** Give people tasks that suit their skills. This not only makes the team more effective but also makes sure that everyone is doing work they feel good about.
- **Team Activities:** Organize activities that help team members learn more about each other's skills and personalities. Whether it's a group project or just a casual lunch, getting to know each other better can make a big difference.
- **Create a Supportive Atmosphere:** Make sure everyone feels that it's okay to admit their weaknesses. When people don't feel judged, they're more likely to speak up about what they need help with, and this can strengthen the team.

- **Celebrate Teamwork:** When you see team members complementing each other's skills, make a point to recognize it. This not only boosts morale but also encourages others to think about how they can work together more effectively.

By putting together, a team where everyone's different skills are valued, you make a workplace where everyone feels they belong and where they can do their best work. It's not about having the perfect team from the start but about growing together and adjusting to make sure everyone can contribute in their own way.

## Who am I?

- I am a professional. Not just because of the job I do but because of how I live every part of my life.
- I am a professional with many visible tattoos. Not to show off but to prove myself that I have patience and courage.
- I am a professional who either wears a messy mom bun or has my hair neatly done. It depends on the day and what it brings.
- I am a professional who makes time to check on my plants even when my schedule is packed. They remind me to take care of myself and the things I love.
- I am a professional who enjoys writing posts. I learn from them and maybe others do too, even if it's just one person reading them.
- I am a professional who is also a daughter, a sister, a wife, a mom, and a friend. Above all, I

am human. Every role teaches me something new and important.

I am still growing. Every day teaches me something. And yes, I am a professional. Even with tattoos on my hands. Even with my old habits. Even with my story still going.

I am a professional in ways that go beyond my job. If you're reading this, you probably are one too. We are more than our titles.

*We are professional dreamers. Let's keep dreaming and keep moving forward.*

### Leadership chose me!

Once, I was scheduled to give a seminar speech in Mumbai. I thought I had plenty of time to prepare, but as days passed, I found myself caught up in work and completely missed out on preparing for the speech. It wasn't until I was at the airport that I realized I wasn't ready at all.

As I boarded the flight and we soared 30,000 feet above the ground, I felt the heat. I grabbed a few tissues and started scribbling notes, trying to gather my thoughts. I felt the pressure knowing this was my first speech in front of a huge crowd.

When I finally walked onto the stage, the sight of the large audience was overwhelming. Despite my lack of preparation, I knew I had to face this challenge head-on. I took a deep breath and started with the first sentence that came to my mind:

"I stood up for myself even before I was born." And continued...

For me Leadership is standing up for yourself even before standing up for others. Well, you can't pour from an empty jar- right?

I'm the youngest daughter of my parents. My mom when she found out she was pregnant, she wanted to get rid of the child as she had been blessed with 2 kids already (my sister & brother) and didn't wanted 3rd one! But God had different plans and so did I ☺

My mom couldn't abort me as it was too late and I made it into this world. Maybe it was God's way of teaching me to stand up for myself even when it's not easy. Naturally I was a stubborn child for my mom then, but now, I'm an apple of her eye, she loves me the most and so do I.

My parents gave me the best of the education and made me independent even before I could think of becoming one. They gave me power through education and prepared me to face the world head-on!

Ultimately my parents injected a mindset into me

*"Don't wait for someone to lead - You take the lead"*

www.ingramcontent.com/pod-product-compliance
Lightning Source LLC
LaVergne TN
LVHW021158160826
845679LV00024B/2150

* 9 7 9 8 8 9 4 7 5 3 5 5 3 *